Revealing Privacy

Margherita Carucci (ed.)

Revealing Privacy

Debating the Understandings of Privacy

PETER LANG
Frankfurt am Main · Berlin · Bern · Bruxelles · New York · Oxford · Wien

Bibliographic Information published by the Deutsche Nationalbibliothek
The Deutsche Nationalbibliothek lists this publication in the Deutsche Nationalbibliografie; detailed bibliographic data is available in the internet at http://dnb.d-nb.de.

Cover Design:
© Olaf Gloeckler, Atelier Platen, Friedberg

ISBN 978-3-631-62128-8

www.peterlang.de

For Charles and Kirsi

A book is the only place in which you can examine a fragile thought without breaking it, or explore an explosive idea without fear it will go off in your face. It is one of the few havens remaining where a man's mind can get both provocation and privacy.

Edward P. Morgan

Table of contents

Editor's Introduction

The papers in this book are versions of a selected number of presentations given at the international symposium 'Revealing Privacy: Debating Understandings of Privacy', that was held at the Helsinki Collegium for Advanced Studies in May 2011. The purpose of this symposium was to bring together a diverse group of scholars from the fields of humanities and social sciences to contribute towards and discuss how privacy is understood today.

Privacy is not a new issue but it remains an enduringly problematic one. In the contemporary world the new means of communication, and the new democratisation of information flows through blogging, twitter, and social networks, have added a distinctive and radical shift to concerns with the boundaries of privacy and its protection. The legal system has historically played a central role in the definition of privacy and its policing. Internationally we can see that different national legal frameworks for the protection of privacy have implications for its maintenance as differing state systems, and their attendant political discourses, frame the understanding and protection of the right to privacy. States and commercial enterprises, for example, increasingly have the capacity and intent to monitor a wide range of our behaviours, from health and mobility, to purchasing habits and internet behaviour. At the same time urban planning is prepared to shape our physical environment in terms of seeking to exclude some citizens and facilitate the participation of others in the interests of a mix of commercial and security rationales: increasingly public space is being privatised. At the same time philosophy and social psychology have engaged in an interrogation of the foundational bases of privacy and its relationship to the construction of the self. Given the dramatic malleability of the experience and the expression of privacy within a specific socio-historical context, these issues remain central to our capacity to enter into any practical concern with the current experience of negotiating privacy in a personal and political space. In the contemporary world, for example, the securitisation of banal daily life is but one of the forces transforming the social, political and legal context within which privacy is negotiated.

The multidimensional character of privacy is reflected in the multiplicity of perspectives from which the contributions in this book approach the topic of privacy. They are, however, united by an interest in promoting further debate. Whether read all together or separately according to the personal interests of the reader, every contribution touches upon the main questions raised by the privacy issue. What is privacy? Is it a right? A privilege? A claim? A condition? A fundamental part of the self? What strategies are used to achieve or to protect the individual's privacy? How are our conceptions of privacy evolved throughout times and cultures?

In 'The private in the public archive', Maryanne Dever discusses the question of how to approach private letters that end up being displayed in the public archive. A private letter is by definition a document containing information that the sender wants to share only with the receiver because of the intimate character of the contents. A personal communication thus reinforces the ties of intimacy between two individuals, and to breach upon it by rendering the letter accessible to others is deemed a violation of privacy. Paradoxically when intimate papers become available for public scrutiny, by virtue of their preservation within an archive, researchers appear to be entitled to read other people's letters and to speculate about their private lives. Whilst the number of specific restrictions dictated by the public archive seems to aim at protecting an individual's rights to privacy, there is doubt whether these archival practices are employed out of concern for the others' privacy. Dever correctly argues that the use of restrictions for the protection of an individual's privacy is rather a means by which to enhance the value of the private document. In this sense, the private contents of a personal letter is the creation of the reader's expectations about the potentially intimate contents of the document.

The intimate character of the personal letters is not questioned when they have been written in earlier times. Rather, they are used as a valuable source of information about general social practices and specific personal thoughts of the writer in a given society. In her paper 'Secrets among spouses: marital privacy in Cicero's letters', Linda McGuire analyses the nature of the private relationship between a husband and a wife in Roman society through a selected number of private letters that the senator Cicero wrote to or about his wife Terentia in the 1st century B.C. While ancient and modern scholarship tends to depict the Roman woman as a powerless individual who was confined within the private space of the house and denied access to public spaces and matters, McGuire's contribution shows that Terentia was a rich and independent woman of the Roman elite and was very capable of acting as intermediary in 'male' financial matters during her husband's exile. In spite of Terentia's financial and moral support, Cicero divorced his wife after thirty years of marriage. This is again a private matter between two spouses but it becomes a topic of public scrutiny and speculation about the reasons of so personal a decision. As McGuire superbly shows throughout her paper, it is difficult to disclose the most private thoughts of a man who employs a number of methods (e.g. nicknames and no discussion of very personal matters) in order to limit potentially dangerous information that may affect his uncertain position as an exile. It is even more difficult to penetrate into the private world of a woman who has no voice in her husband's letters. As in most marriages ending with divorce, there was probably a problem of communication between Cicero and Terentia, which could be related to two main factors: the long distance, which physically separated the husband from his wife, and the lack of a house as a materially defined space where the two spouses could share intimacy and protect personal information from public scrutiny and interference. Also, because of the loss of his house as the physical space traditionally associated with the woman in her role as a wife and a mother, Cicero would have found it more difficult to locate his wife Terentia.

The topic of domestic privacy in the Roman house is discussed in my contribution 'Visualising ancient privacy in the Roman house'. Any discussion on the meaning and experience of domestic privacy in ancient times is fraught with difficulties. Few of the Latin writers speak of themselves or of their characters as seeking or enjoying privacy. Yet some of their works reveal dramatic tensions between the need for retreat and community, for concealment and visibility, for intimacy and self-presentation: the fundamental conflict between privacy and publicity. This tension also appears in the spatial arrangement of the Roman house: spaces designed for the reception of the house-owner's guests (public areas) are placed side by side with spaces for the personal use of the family (private rooms). The paper shows how in their everyday practices the Romans negotiated the harms and expectations of informational and spatial privacy through a selection of specific moments for exposure or concealment.

The social analysis of ancient communities is certainly fraught with many difficulties not only because of the distance in time but also for the lack of ample documentation about how people experienced their houses or what their innermost feelings and thoughts were. By contrast, anthropological fieldwork in existent communities gives the great advantage of obtaining first-hand material through observation, however difficult it may be for the anthropologist to interact with people from a different cultural background. The results of participant observation thus open up new paths of investigation and allow a deeper understanding of universal phenomena such as privacy. This is evident in Elena Liarskaia and Stephan Dudeck's paper on 'Multiple privacies – Nesting spheres of intimacy in Western Siberian indigenous lifestyles'. The two scholars argue that, in spite of the lack of the term 'privacy' in the language of two indigenous communities in Western Siberia, their social practices show an idea of what in the Western culture we call privacy and intimacy. This appears in the way the members of these communities set boundaries around specific knowledge of the self in order to protect their integrity and to show their respect of pre-existing norms of behaviour in the community to which they belong. The disclosure of inappropriate information about the individual or the display of practices that should be kept hidden, such as sexual intercourse or the woman's unveiling of her head, cause shame and embarrassment. The result is not the individual's concealment of information or secrecy but the public avoidance of knowledge that can harm the reputation of that individual. The practices of these communities thus show different sensibilities toward the private sphere of their members.

There is no doubt that values of, and approaches to, privacy are affected by the individual's relation with the community and the physical space where both individual and community are located, may it be a natural setting or a small village or a larger city. The dimension of privacy within the specific urban experience is discussed in two contributions: 'Sociological and philosophical insight into privacy in postmodern cities' by Karol Kurnicki and Katarzyna Salamon; 'Privacy and depth configurations. Proximity, permeability and territorial boundaries in urban projects' by Kris Scheerlinck.

Kurnicki and Salamon argue that the personal and social experience of the inhabitant of the urban space in post-modern times is affected by the lack of a clear distinction between the public and the private. Since the 5th century BC Western philosophical theories about the relation of the individual with the community have been based on the dual role of the person as private in relation to herself and public in relation to the society. In the post-modern city, by contrast, privacy is mainly associated with the idea of personal security achieved through the social control of the space. The result is the creation of a gated community as a defensive measure against the threats of violation of the community outside. However, the control of access into this closed space limits the possibility of encounters with non-residents and therefore occasions of communal life. Kurnicki and Snell suggest that a renewed demarcation between public and private would enhance the social and personal experience of the person.

By contrast, Kris Sheerlinck states that the relation between public and private spaces in the urban projects is mediated by the collective spaces. The variety of the forms and characters of the collective spaces, may they be located in the restricted area of a domestic building or in the wider context of an urban area, depends on the multiplicity of depth configurations. The concept of depth configuration refers to the arrangement of a sequence of movements between public and private spaces. Depending on the number of sequences and the ways buildings or areas are accessed, privacy is achieved when the individual has the possibility of deciding where and when she does not want to share space.

Concerns with the boundaries of privacy and its protection have been dramatically increased with the development of media technologies, such as photography and social networks. In her contribution 'Privacy, photography, and the art defense', Sarah Parson discusses privacy concerns raised by specific practices of photography for the uncertainly defined purposes of social activism or artistic expression. When used as a visual documentation of the social conditions of those categories of people kept outside the frame of public visibility and recognition, photography surely contributes to public opinion and debate. However, the wide circulation in public spaces of photos illustrating private moments of an individual's life inevitably raises the question as to whether her privacy is protected. The question becomes more urgent when those photos are sold at high price and the photographer gets benefits in terms of material reward and popularity. The private life of the individual portrayed in those photos becomes an object for public consumption. Does this use of photography as a means of social activism justify the potential violation of intimacy of private persons? Does the exhibition of these photos in art galleries make this use of photography a superior form of artistic expression? How can these photos sold in a commercial gallery differ from the photos used for more immediately commercial purposes like, for example, the photos of celebrities sold by paparazzi to tabloids? To reply to these questions is not an easy task. As Parsons superbly argues, 'we need to acknowledge the complexity of the issue' before any attempt to develop a theoretical framework explaining the relation between photography and privacy.

This complexity of the privacy issue seems to be mainly related to the great ambiguity in the way people limit access to personal information or have the right to control information about themselves. Theoretically, the people's ability to restrict or to share the flow of appropriate information about themselves provides a kind of reassurance that their privacy is protected. But how can this form of information be controlled in cyberspace, where the circulation of information does not seem to be regulated by any well defined norm? What kind of personal information is deemed as appropriate for circulation in social networking sites? These questions are being widely debated in current thinking about informational privacy and many theories are being formulated.

In 'Social networking sites and privacy as contextual integrity', Miia Vistilä and Floora Ruokonen discuss one of these formulations, i.e. the theory of contextual integrity. The normative account of privacy holds that the distribution or flow of information in a specific context is to be regulated by norms that establish what kind of information is appropriate or inappropriate in that context. When norms of appropriateness internal to context or when norms of information flow across contexts have been disrupted, a violation of privacy occurs. But how can privacy claims be justified in the context of social networks, where the norms of appropriateness are not clearly articulated and the reasonable expectations of privacy are based on the normative appropriateness borrowed from other contexts? Vistilä and Ruokonen correctly argue that the novelty of social networking experience demands the formulation of specific norms that can guide the user toward a better understanding of what kind of information and expectations are appropriate in the context of communication technology for the protection of her and others' privacy. This goal may prove to be a difficult one to achieve, given the continuous changes of people's approaches to social networks: while getting more familiar with, or more dependent on, internet communication, the person changes the way to see and recognise herself and others. Notwithstanding, the formulation of some norms would help the members of the virtual communities have a more positive social experience without the constant feeling of the impending threat of privacy violation. In spite of their virtual character, social networks offer an immediate space for the individual's presentation of the self and for the relation of this specific self with a wider community.

The issue of informational privacy in relation to the individual's self-reflection and self-presentation in virtual communities is discussed by Ilpo Helén and Karoliina Snell in their contribution on 'Private life in bits and pieces: Digital and molecular personhood in the information age'. Here focus is on a specific form of informational privacy, i.e. medical data stored and circulated in biobank networks. The highly private character of health and genomic data makes the individual particularly sensitive to problems related to the protection of her personal privacy from intrusion. The focus group interviews conducted by Helén and Snell show the generally positive approach of the individual toward the circulation of her medical information for future research studies, believing that personal data stored in the biobanks are only used for biomedical research. However, as for all pieces of personal information circulating in cyberspace, may they be in the context of social networks or biobanks, the individual is left with the unpleasant feeling that she cannot have full control of the information flows, once they are turned into a digitalised form. The lack of transparency in the entire World Wide Web thus becomes the most immediate threat of privacy violation. Does it essentially matter whether the potential violation of the person's privacy occurs in the popular social networks or in the socially useful biobanks?

In conclusion, there is neither conclusion nor the definitive formulation of a theoretical model that can be widely applied in any discourse on privacy. The variety and complexity of meanings of privacy reflects the multifaceted aspects of human experience, which cannot be easily explored within a single framework for interpretation. This book gives the reader the great opportunity to explore some of these aspects and to learn more about privacy - how important it is to us and how much we will miss it if it is neglected – and ultimately more about ourselves.

The private in the public archive

Maryanne Dever

Abstract

Distinctions between public and private — however problematic and contested — turn on notions of borders or boundaries and this essay examines approaches to collections of private and, in some cases, highly personal papers that have found their way into public repositories. These private/public papers possess different qualities and pose different challenges from those associated with preserving and researching administrative or government records. I ask what makes an archived document 'private'? What protocols govern scholarly access to these particular elements of the archival record? Finally, and more significantly, what are the effects of this categorization? I conclude by considering how the productivity of the 'private' may be bound up with questions of value.

Mercedes de Acosta's papers in the Rosenbach Library and Museum in Philadelphia contain a series of letters written to her by the screen star Greta Garbo.[1] Among them is one sent in 1950 from Indio, east of Palm Springs, where Garbo had retreated for a few weeks to stay with her close friend, George Schlee. The letter carries a series of anxious instructions to de Acosta concerning how she was to reply. She must address her reply only to Schlee (not to Garbo) in order to minimise the risk of revealing her whereabouts. At the same time, she must be sure to glue the envelope well to prevent prying eyes from discovering the contents. The irony is that this letter – with all Garbo's palpable concern for concealing her identity and whereabouts – is now on open access to readers. It is well-established that de Acosta sold the Garbo letters to the Rosenbach in 1960 as part of her accumulated personal archive, a decision prompted by her increasingly precarious financial situation. The letters were restricted (in this instance they were closed both to researchers and to staff) from the date of their accession until 15 April 2000 – ten years from the date of Garbo's death. On that day, the world's press carried breathless accounts of the curators cutting the red ribbons that had encircled the box of letters. I want to use the letter I have just described (or the case of the Greta Garbo correspondence at the Rosenbach more generally) not as an illustration so much as a provocation: to examine a series of questions about the status of the 'private' document – and, in particular, restricted personal correspondence – in the public archive. I want to ask: what makes an archived document 'private',

1 Mercedes de Acosta Papers, Rosenbach Museum and Library, Philadelphia, PA. Greta Garbo material 1197/8, Box 23, Folder 30.

what are the effects of this categorisation, and how is the private bound up with questions of value?

Distinctions are generally made by those in the field between public records – that is, official documents or data generated by organizations in the course of their formal operations – and personal papers – letters, diaries, notes, photographs, and other ephemera generated by individuals in the course of living their lives. Such papers, in contrast to public records, may reflect no obvious order or system, just as they may display no purposive intent beyond the (selective) witnessing of a life as lived. Canadian archivist Catherine Hobbs refers to such papers as 'the flotsam of the individual life', noting that there exists 'an intimacy in the personal archive not present in the collective, corporate, formalized record-keeping system'.[2] Some archived collections of personal papers may be the result of considered decision-making on the part of a donor, as in the case of living authors who benefit financially from the sale or donation of archivable materials, whose donations both anticipate and incite critical interest in their work, and who can and do exercise their proprietary right of ownership to shape and winnow materials with a keen eye to posterity. Robert McGill makes the point that

> …living authors read criticism and respond to it, they give interviews or refuse to give them, they defend or relinquish their right to privacy, they create archives in anticipation of critical interest, they support themselves through selling archival materials in a market made buoyant by biographical desire, and they destroy materials they do not want critics to view. Jonathan Franzen observes of these last actions, 'I…don't see how you resist the temptation to select material that suggests the most flattering possible narratives. And not just select, but actively create!'[3]

But in addition to those materials that have been carefully lodged there by design, archives are also filled with what historian Carolyn Steedman so colourfully terms the 'mad fragmentations that no one intended to preserve and that just ended up there'.[4]

Discussion of privacy in the realm of publicly accessible records is increasingly focused on what we might term 'information ethics', with debate driven by the search for appropriate and uniform protocols to govern the proliferation of banks of personal data in the global digital environment.[5] But the issues that shape those debates – questions of consent, storage and access – are the same questions faced by those tasked with the acquisition, preservation

---

2 Hobbs 2001, 127, 131.

3 McGill 2009, 142.

4 Steedman 1998, 67.

5 See, for example, Cambon-Thomsen 2004; Craig 2005; MacNeil 1992; Sturges 2009; Todd 2006; Waldby 1997.

and on-going management of personal papers held in the public domain.[6] The acquisition and preservation of personal papers within public collections is inevitably undertaken with a view to their use by an imagined future public and for this reason, as Heather MacNeil asserts, while professional archivists working in this area 'do not dispute the significance of individual rights to privacy, they are more inclined to publicly promote the importance and value of increased accessibility to archival holdings'.[7] Libraries and archives are usually reluctant to accept collections – no matter how valuable – that are to be permanently closed to even the most limited forms of public scrutiny for their role is then reduced to that of a mere storage facility.

In Panofsky and Moir's analysis, this reluctance derives at least in part from the practical (and fiscal) reality that collecting institutions

> invest significant time, energy, and financial resources into acquiring archival collections and ensuring their preservation through the use of specialized supplies, through labour-intensive conservation treatments for select items, and by establishing environmentally controlled storage facilities ... [it is] far more expensive to manage a linear metre of archival holdings than to manage the equivalent amount of published material on a library's open shelves. A reasonable return on this investment can be achieved only through unfettered access to and use of archival collections.[8]

For this reason, institutions are more likely to seek to work with donors to establish informed consent to the placing of their personal papers in the public domain, albeit sometimes with a range of specified restrictions. For example, donors may request the right to screen researchers before granting permission to access, copy and/or cite papers. Others may make arrangements to keep the whole or parts of a collection closed to all readers for fixed periods of time or until a particular event (e.g. the death of the donor or subject of the papers). In the case of Mercedes de Acosta, elements of her collection were not to be made publicly available until a decade after the death of the individuals associated with the different portions of the papers. This would appear to be a reasonable and workable arrangement, unlike the oft-cited and seemingly arbitrary

---

6 See, for example, Panofsky and Moir 2005; Hodson 2004; Behrnd-Klodt and Wosh 2005.

7 MacNeil 2005, 68. By way of example, the Society of American Archivists (SAA) Code of Ethics includes the following: 'Archivists recognize their responsibility to promote the use of records as a fundamental purpose of the keeping of archives. Archivists may place restrictions on access for the protection of privacy or confidentiality of information in the records'. Source: http://www2.archivists.org/standards/code-of-ethics-for-archivists. Accessed 21 December 2011.

8 Panofsky and Moir 2005, 25.

restrictions governing unspecified sections of the James Joyce correspondence held in the National Library of Ireland which are closed until 2050 (more than a century after Joyce's death) or the infamous Series Z of the Freud Collection in the Library of Congress which is embargoed until the twenty-second century or the year 2113 to be precise.[9] Whatever form they take, these policies and practices are designed to encourage donors to save and give – rather than withhold and possibly destroy – sensitive or revealing materials 'that can make it possible for all of us to ask new questions about the past'.[10]

But while donors are usually afforded ample opportunity to outline their sensitivities and concerns in this regard, third parties to collections can be denied this by virtue of being unaware that their papers are to be publicly deposited. This is most often the case with correspondence where it is routinely the recipient not the sender who retains possession, asserts ownership and can therefore exercise the right to dispose of the physical document as she or he chooses. The recipient's capacity to determine the fate of the physical letter means personal information, opinions, and insights conveyed to someone in confidence can readily find their way into the public domain without the author's knowledge or consent. If we take the example of the love letters from novelist J.D. Salinger to Joyce Maynard with whom he had had a brief relationship in 1972-73. Maynard's decision in 1999 to sell the fourteen letters she had received from the reclusive Salinger generated considerable publicity as journalists debated what they referred to erroneously as the 'private rights of public figures'.[11] However, it was acknowledged throughout the ensuing media storm that Maynard as owner/recipient had a legal right to dispose of the physical letters.[12] Codes of practice for professional archivists in different national domains routinely contain some reference to respecting 'the privacy of individuals who created or are the subjects of records, especially those who had no voice in the use or disposition of the materials'.[13] Such codes, however, generally offer no explicit guidelines as to how this might be achieved, leading to considerable varia-

9 Sax 1999, 127. See also Malcolm 1984.

10 Schwarz 2005, 83.

11 Applebome 1999.

12 The 14 letters sold through Sotheby's for $156,500 to a retired Californian software millionaire who promised to return them to the reclusive author. See Gardiner 1999. Another more recent and complicated case involves French novelist Patrick Poivre D'Arvor who was sued by his former partner, Agathe Borne, for allegedly publishing her love letters in his novel, *Fragments of a Lost Woman* (2009). See Bremmer 2011.

13 This example is drawn from VSA - Verein Schweizerischer Archivarinnen und Archivare: Code of Ethics (2005). Emphasis added.

tion in practice. The Bodleian Library at Oxford, for example, automatically restricts all correspondence from living persons in its various collections.[14] Still others, cognizant of the fact that individuals retain copyright in the text of the letters they write, rely on them to use that avenue to suppress publication of materials they do not wish to see in circulation. Indeed, this was the strategy earlier used by J.D. Salinger to prevent biographer Ian Hamilton from quoting from or even paraphrasing any of Salinger's letters that had been donated to university libraries where – to his dismay – they were freely available to researchers.[15] All distinctions between public and private – however problematic and contested – turn on some notion of a border or boundary,[16] and the one that is routinely invoked here is that between what is (or should be) publicly accessible and what is not.

If we look at these attempts to manage access to personal papers in public collections, it is interesting that the policies do not define what constitutes the 'private'. This assumes that the private is either a consensus state requiring no elaboration or a self-evident quality that simply inheres in the documents in question. Of the former proposition, I would suggest that far from consensus, there is a fair degree of slippage in many discussions of archiving and accessing personal correspondence between notions of the private, the intimate, the secret and the potentially embarrassing or scandalous. The latter proposition, meanwhile, relies on an idea of the archive as a mere repository of inert documents whose meaning is fixed and fully-present, something that has been radically questioned now through a whole series of critical interventions that have transformed understandings of 'the archive' as a cultural institution.[17] Yet, what if we consider that rather than a pre-existing state or an inherent condition, 'the private' is in fact the effect of the promise of something that can be brought into being through the very archival practices designed to manage and protect it?

I want to return here to the Greta Garbo letters at the Rosenbach. Garbo is perhaps an appropriate figure around whom to speculate on questions of privacy given she was renowned for her reclusive tendencies and her famous demand to be 'let alone'.[18]

---

14 Sax 1999, 119.

15 See Hamilton 1988 for his response to this blocking of access.

16 See, for example, Weintraub and Kumar 1997.

17 Burton 2005; Dever, Newman and Vickery 2009; Derrida 2002; Foucault 1972; Osborne 1999; Steedman 2002.

18 Garbo is often misquoted as saying 'I want to be alone'. However, she was at pains to clarify that what she said was, 'I want to be let alone'. The misquote is parodied by her character, the prima ballerina Grusinskaya, in the film *Grand Hotel* (1932).

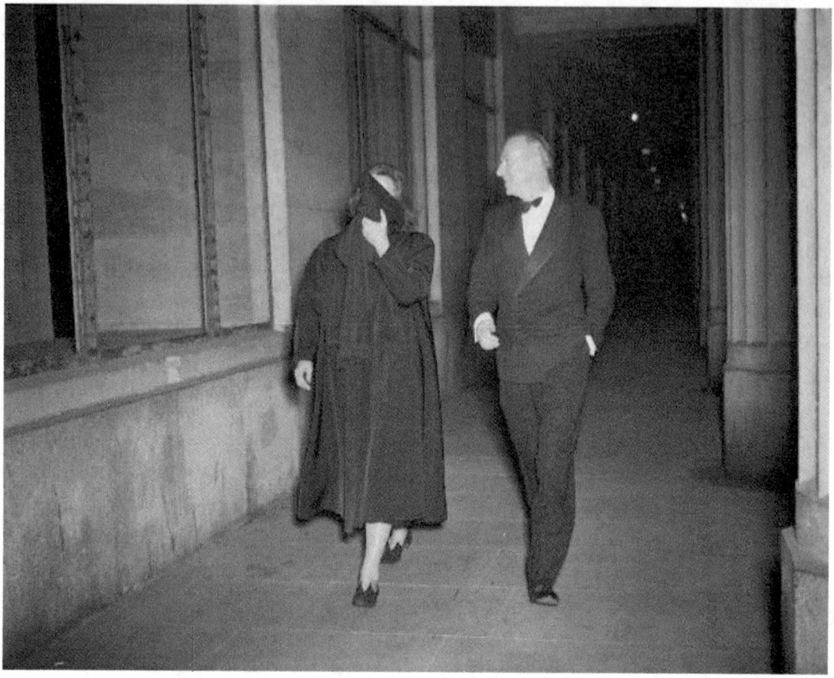

Fig.: *Swedish actress Greta Garbo (1905 - 1990) hides her face with her handbag as she leaves an election night reception at the Savoy Hotel, London with British photographer Cecil Beaton (1904 - 1980), 26th October 1951. (Photo by George W. Hales/Fox Photos/Hulton Archive. Courtesy of Getty Images.)*

As a star, she refused invitations to both private social engagements and public events, avoided signing autographs, seldom agreed to interviews and arranged to have her fan mail burned unopened. While her insistence on privacy in the publicity seeking world of 1920s and 1930s Hollywood has been interpreted more recently as arising from a wish to suppress speculation about her personal life, it has also been suggested that it revealed a keen understanding of the counter-value of inaccessibility in a world of otherwise available stars: in short, it was a calculated strategy designed 'to create an aura of mystery that elevated her above other glamorous but more accessible stars'.[19] Inaccessibility fueled the desire to know her and to know more about her. Viewed in this way, it might be argued that it was the quality of inaccessibility that produced the idea of Garbo as a 'private' person and not vice versa. What if we hold that

19 Gever 2003, 129.

observation, and move forward several decades to consider the situation of Garbo's letters to Mercedes de Acosta.

Few people probably even knew of the letters' existence before the world's media began to track the story of the closed collection in the lead up to the scheduled opening in April 2000. Press coverage centred on the fact that the letters were presumed to be love letters ('letter bombs'[20]) and it was widely speculated in the media that their release would finally confirm a rumoured liaison between Garbo and de Acosta (the 'smoking lipstick'[21]). The publicising of a planned exhibition at the Rosenbach entitled 'Garbo Unsealed' which was to showcase a selection of the letters no doubt added to the sense of anticipation and pending revelation. Original archival documents already possess a particular aura that derives from their rarity or their 'unique existence'.[22] This is, after all, what gives them their value both in strictly market terms[23] and as objects of attraction or desire for readers and researchers. The restricting of access to such papers only adds further to their aura by endowing them with an additional set of assumed properties, in this instance with the promise of intimate disclosure and enhanced prurient value. When these properties align they can in turn generate even greater market value as demonstrated by the offering for sale of 66 letters from actress Elizabeth Taylor to her first fiancé, William Pawley, the son of a former US ambassador. Those letters had been privately held by Pawley – and thus neither seen nor accessible – from 1949 until two years ago when they were quietly secured by the RR Auction firm. The online auction which was timed to extract maximum benefit from the global coverage of the star's recent passing promoted the fact that this was an 'unprecedented, one–of–a–kind collection' containing 'the never-before-seen...revealing letters that chronicle 17-year-old Elizabeth Taylor's first love'.[24] The tantalizing promise not only of the singular and the original — but also and crucially — of the not-yet-seen, the something

20 Carrie Rickey in the Philadelphia Inquirer, 19 March 2000. Cited in Paris 2000a.

21 Paris 2000b.

22 Benjamin 1968, 221. Coverage in Britain's *The Daily Mail* in April 2011 of the sale of an original autograph letter from the young Norma Jean Baker (Marilyn Monroe) to her foster mother elicited the following on-line contribution from a reader: 'The fact that this letter sold for so much and is still newsworthy after all this time shows what a 'one off' she was'. This suggests that the aura of the singular and original is shared here both by the letter and its author. See Anon 2011.

23 On this point, see Browar 2002.

24 Item 645: Elizabeth Taylor. R.R Auction (America's Autograph Auction). Emphasis added. See: http://www.rrauction.com/past_auction_item.cfm?ID=3234567. Accessed 21 December 2011. The letters sold on 19 May 2011 for US$47, 652.

apparently 'there' in the letters to be revealed or found, generates a similar aura to that surrounding the restricted or closed archival holding.

Such was the power of the aura surrounding the long-closed Garbo documents that it produced on the part of the Garbo estate a frantic excursion into the performative: Gray Reisfield Horan, Garbo's grand-niece with responsibility for her literary estate attended the private opening ceremony, together with official biographer, Karen Swenson, as privileged initial readers of the newly unsealed correspondence. It is ironic — but perhaps in terms of what I am arguing here not entirely surprising — that after the long build up the opening of the Rosenbach letters was reported in the press under headlines such as 'Garbo papers reveal nothing'.[25] Horan and Swenson made statements indicating that they found the letters to contain nothing compelling by way of 'evidence' as to the nature of the relationship between the two women: 'there [was] no concrete evidence that any sexual relationship between these two women ever existed'.[26] While I have elsewhere questioned the hermeneutic certainty of those statements,[27] my interest here is in the productive effects of the sequestering of the papers: how it generated the promise of something private and unseen, a sense not of what the papers are but what they can do. This drew Horan and Swenson to the opening just as surely as it later drew me to the Rosenbach's reading room: a testament to the fact that the auratic power or promise associated with these papers continues even after the restrictions that produced it have long since been lifted. Horan and Swenson were consumed by concern for what the papers might come to mean as the process of restricting access had endowed them with potential. In this way, their hasty reading of and reporting on the letters can be understood as an attempt to arrest and close down that potential.

But if the 'private' can be understood as an effect of particular archival practices, the Garbo letters also point to the way in which the private and, by extension, its protection — something so often positioned as a benign moral imperative — is inevitably entangled with questions of value. Alison Moore, in a parallel discussion of restrictions governing 'licentious' books, makes the point that such formal hurdles are 'only partially about limiting access'; they are also about the creation of meaning and value for such cultural artefacts.[28] For example, now that the Garbo letters are unsealed and may be read at the Rosenbach Museum and Library, the Garbo literary estate, controlled by Gray Horan, does

25 Anon 2000.

26 Anon 2000.

27 See Dever 2010.

28 Moore 2007.

not grant permission for the letters to be quoted directly:[29] a continuing restriction designed to protect and enhance the current (and future) value of the product that is the enduring image or brand of Garbo. Corresponding interpretations have been made of the prolonged closure of elements of the Freud papers held in the Library of Congress, with various scholars suggesting the embargoes are designed to forestall critical or hostile readings considered potentially damaging to Freud's legacy by the directors of the Freud Archive.[30] In short, the closure or restriction of papers participates in the on-going reputational work that is intimately connected to the creation of value in and through those papers.

Far from being a benign set of protocols for managing access to particular sets of documents, restrictions aimed at protecting 'private' documents in public archives establish the very conditions under which these documents can come to mean and through which their value may be both built and leveraged. Recognising the productivity of those protocols raises important methodological challenges for those involved in working with archival sources, not least because it forces us to reconsider the status of the archive itself and to question what archives are, what they can do, and the role of futurity or potential in our archival logic. In particular, we must confront the fact that if archiving produces as much as it records any person or event,[31] then it is through the work of anticipation and in unactualised possibilities that the 'private' must be understood.

Bibliography

Anon, 2000. 'Briefs'. *The Age* (Melbourne) 16 April, 11.

Anon, 2011.' "He keeps me busy cooking and cleaning": Letter penned by Marilyn Monroe at 16 reveals her early life as a desperate housewife'. *The Daily Mail* 22 April. http://www.dailymail.co.uk/tvshowbiz/article-1379365/He-keeps-busy-cleaning-house-fixing-meals-Letter-penned-Marilyn-Monroe-16-reveals-early-life-desperate-housewife.html. Retrieved: 20/4/12.

Applebome, P. 1999. 'Love letters in the wind: A private affair of the famously private Salinger'. *The New York Times* 12 May.

Behrnd-Klodt, M. L. and Wosh, P. J. (eds.) 2005. *Privacy and confidentiality perspectives: Archivists and archival records*. Chicago: The Society of American Archivists.

Benjamin, W. 1968. 'The work of art in the age of mechanical reproduction'. In H. Arendt (ed.) *Illuminations: Essays and Reflections*. Trans. H. Zohn. New York: Schocken, 217-51.

29 See Schanke n.d.

30 For a brief account, see Sax 1999, 129-33.

31 See Derrida 2002, 17.

Bremmer, C. 2011.'French author Patrick Poivre d'Arvor sued for literary theft after he prints private love letters'. *The Times* 9 June.

Browar, L. 2002. 'Pushing paper: Dealers and institutional collectors'. *Libraries & Culture*, 37.1, 53-6.

Burton, A. (ed.) 2005. *Archive stories: Facts, fictions, and the writing of history*. Durham: Duke University Press.

Cambon-Thomsen, A. 2004. 'The social and ethical issues of post-genomic human biobanks'. *Nature Reviews Genetics*, 5, 866-73.

Craig, B. L. 2005. 'Confidences in medical and health care records from an archive perspective'. In M. L. Behrnd-Klodt and P. J. Wosh (eds.) *Privacy and confidentiality perspectives: Archivists and archival records.* Chicago: The Society of American Archivists, 246-56.

Derrida, J. 2002. *Archive fever: A Freudian impression*. Trans. Eric Prenowitz. Chicago: The University of Chicago Press.

Dever, M., Newman, S. and Vickery, A. 2009. *The intimate archive: Journeys through private papers*. Canberra: The National Library of Australia.

Dever, M. 2010. 'Greta Garbo's foot or sex, socks and letters'. *Australian Feminist Studies*, 25.64, 163-74.

Foucault, M. 1972. *The archaeology of knowledge*. Trans. A.M. Sheridan Smith. London: Tavistock.

Gardiner, B. 1999. 'Salinger's letters to Maynard sell for $156,500'. *The Columbian* (Vancouver, WA), 23 June.

Gever, M. 2003. *Entertaining lesbians: Celebrity, sexuality, and self-invention.* New York and London: Routledge.

Hamilton, I. 1988. *In search of J.D. Salinger*. London: Heinemann.

Hobbs, C. 2001. 'The character of personal archives: Reflections on the value of records of individuals'. *Archivaria*, 52, 126-35.

Hodson, S. S. 2004. 'In silence sealed: Privacy in the papers of authors and celebrities'. *The American Archivist*, 67.2, 194-211.

MacNeil, H. 1992. *Without consent: The ethics of disclosing personal information in public archives*. Metuchen, N.J. and London: The Society of American Archivists and the Scarecrow Press, Inc.

MacNeil, H. 2005. 'Privacy, liberty and democracy'. In M. L. Behrnd-Klodt and P. J. Wosh (eds.) *Privacy and confidentiality perspectives: Archivists and archival records*. Chicago: The Society of American Archivists, 67-81.

Malcolm, J. 1984. *In the Freud Archives*. New York: Knopf.

McGill, R. 2009. 'Biographical desire and the archives of living authors'. *a/b: Autobiography Studies*, 24.1, 129-45.

Moore, A. 2007. 'Access and exclusion, obstruction and protection in the guarding of licentious books'. Paper presented at the Bodies of Knowledge: Archives and Sexuality Conference, University of Queensland, 26-28 April.

Osborne, T. 1999. 'The ordinariness of the archive'. *History of the Human Sciences*, 12.2, 51-64.

Panofsky R. and Moir, M. 2005. 'Halted by the archive: The impact of excessive archival restrictions on scholars'. *Journal of Scholarly Publishing*, 37.1, 19-32.

Paris, B. 2000a. 'Letter bombs? Museum will open Garbo's correspondence to alleged socialite lover'. *Pittsburgh Post-Gazette*, 13 April.

Paris, B. 2000b. 'Mercedes and Garbo: Read between the lines'. *Pittsburgh Post-Gazette*, 24 April.

Sax, J. L., 1999. *Playing darts with a Rembrandt: Public and private rights in cultural treasures*. Ann Arbor: The University of Michigan Press.

Schanke, R. n.d. 'Mercedes de Acosta'. www.robertschanke.com/mercedes/loves.htm. Retrieved: 16/10/11.

Schwarz, J. 2005. 'The archivist's balancing act: Helping researchers while protecting individual privacy'. In M. L. Behrnd-Klodt and P. J. Wosh (eds.) *Privacy and confidentiality perspectives: Archivists and archival records*. Chicago: The Society of American Archivists, 82-92.

Steedman, C. 1998. 'The space of memory: In an archive'. *History of the Human Sciences*, 11.4, 65-84.

Steedman, C. 2002. Dust: *The archive and cultural history*. New Brunswick, NJ: Rutgers University Press.

Sturges, P. 2009. 'Information ethics in the twenty-first century'. *Australian Academic & Research Libraries*, 40.4, 241-51.

Todd, M. 2006. 'Power, identity, authenticity, and the archives: A comparative study of the application of archival methodologies to contemporary privacy'. *Archivaria*, 6, 181-214.

Waldby, C. 1997. 'The body and the digital archive: The visible human project and the computerization of medicine'. *Health: An Interdisciplinary Journal for the Social Study of Health, Illness, and Medicine*, 1.2, 227-42.

Weintraub, J. and Kumar, K. (eds.) 1997. *Public and private in thought and practice*. Chicago: Chicago University Press.

Secrets among spouses: marital privacy in Cicero's letters

Linda McGuire

Abstract

In elite Roman families, women played several key roles in marriage. First, they could act as pawns to seal political alliances with other families. Second, they were often a source of wealth for impecunious men from respectable families wishing to advance socially. Cicero's marriage to Terentia gave him access to a dowry of HS 400,000, which was the wealth qualification required to become a senator (Plutarch, *Life of Cicero*, 8). Her dowry also provided him with an annual income of HS 80,000 allowing him to start building a career in the law courts without having to worry about earning money himself. Cicero's correspondence highlights his role in politics – indeed it has been suggested that the letters were chosen by his editor for that very purpose. The more than 900 letters selected and published after his death are unique in that they reveal, at least to some extent, the private thoughts of a very public figure. This is particularly true of the volume of letters he wrote to his close friend and confidant Titus Pomponius, known to everyone as Atticus. The idea of privacy pervades his letters to Atticus in his obsession with their safe delivery and in the different ways he attempts to obscure his opinions about others except to the addressee. What can they tell a modern reader about the idea of privacy in Roman marriage? For instance, Terentia managed a vast fortune, successfully by some accounts, that was legally separate from her husband's property. How much involvement did she have in Cicero's personal financial affairs according to his letters? Also, how much access would she have had to his correspondence (both received and sent)? And how does she generally appear in letters not addressed directly to her? This paper does not want to suggest that they were a typical married couple. However, in view of ancient writers' glorification of elite women who devoted themselves entirely to domestic affairs, and modern assumptions that little affection existed in these quasi-arranged marriages, this question might cast some light on relations between husbands and wives in the ancient world.

Raymond Wacks suggests that one of the main concerns about privacy lies in our need to protect sensitive information.[1] In ancient Rome, marriage was a private act requiring no official recognition by a governmental or religious body.[2] Much less is known of the concept of privacy within a marriage and what information would have been considered too sensitive to divulge to a spouse. It is generally understood today that among the Roman elite marriage was a largely political affair. It was for creating political alliances, enhancing the social standing of your family or attaining the property requirements to advance in your career. Spouses are understood as having a business-like relationship and the busi-

1 Wacks 2010, x.
2 Veyne 1985, 45.

ness was high politics.[3] On the surface Cicero's marriage to Terentia seems to fit this criteria.[4] In many ways she was the perfect candidate for marriage for an unknown and ambitious politician for what she brought to it – respectable money. Yet what about the day-to-day dynamics of such arrangements? This paper will focus on the idea of marital privacy in terms of information shared between husband and wife or in some cases not shared.[5] The main source used will be Cicero's personal letters to his close friend Atticus, where Terentia plays a relatively minor role, plus the handful of surviving letters to her. The letters will be examined for their contents, Terentia's appearance in them and her access to them. What can this approach tell us about Cicero's marriage in relation to Roman concepts of an ideal wife? A secondary aim will be to challenge the rather negative reputation that Terentia has acquired as a domineering and ambitious woman.[6]

The source material

Cicero, like many of his social group (both male and female), was an avid letter writer. Of the 931 letters that were collected and published after his death in 43 BC, 426 were addressed to Atticus and 24 to his wife Terentia.[7] The letters date from when Cicero was 38 years old until the year before his death at the age of 63 and they cover the two most traumatic periods of Cicero's political career: his exile in 58-57 BC and the period of 48-47 BC when he was a political outcast in the civil war between Julius Caesar and Pompey the Great. Cicero's letters are unique in that he never intended to publish them (at least in their current form), unlike the letters of Pliny the Younger and Seneca, making them an extremely important source to examine the private thoughts of a prominent figure.[8]

3 For some general background on the relationship between husbands and wives, Hallett 1984 and Dixon 1991. Saxonhouse (1992) discusses expectations towards women in public and private realms.

4 Marcus Tullius Cicero (106-43 BC) was a leading Roman senator and orator whose surviving works include speeches, philosophical writings and private letters.

5 Riggsby 1997, 48 defines the term privacy in ancient Rome. For privacy in the Roman house, see Riggsby 1997, Grahame 1997 and Margherita Carucci's paper in this collection.

6 Plutarch, *Life of Cicero* 21; 29.

7 The editor chose from a larger selection and tried to focus on politics, White 2010, ix-x.

8 Pliny the Younger, Roman senator and prefect of the state treasury under Emperor Trajan, is well known for his surviving collection of letters. A number of literary and philosophical works survive of Lucius Annaeus Seneca (4 – 65 AD), senator and former tutor

Indeed, that he was an intensely private man comes across clearly in this body of correspondence and this ran into direct conflict with his need to communicate openly with Atticus during long periods of separation. Cicero employed a number of methods to ensure safe delivery of his letters. He tried to use only letter carriers he trusted.[9] He sometimes refrained from using names or gave people nicknames of his own invention.[10] The two friends mainly avoided discussing delicate political matters as well as some personal ones such as a disagreement between Cicero's brother and Atticus.[11] Of course what was shared between the two men would not have been the same as between husband and wife.

Financial support

Terentia provided Cicero with a sufficient dowry to be eligible for election as a senator and an annual income.[12] Outside her dowry, their finances remained separate, as she would have retained ownership and control of any property or assets inherited from her family.[13] This separation of spousal property was further underlined in laws banning the exchange of gifts of any value between husband and wife.[14] Given this legal situation, it might be expected that money was not discussed between spouses. Yet the contents of his letters show the opposite to be true. This section will argue that she had considerable involvement in his financial affairs by looking at several different services she provided.

First, it appears that she was expected to carry out financial transactions for him while he was away from Rome. His friends Camillus and Atticus were in charge of managing his wealth and the freedman Philotimus did the legwork.[15] Terentia seems to have acted mainly as an intermediary. In one example, she helps to see that he is provided with money while he is stuck in Brundisium awaiting the pardon of Julius Caesar. Letter 11.11 describes how Cicero is supplied money locally by a man named Gn Sallustius. He arranges for Atticus in

of Emperor Nero. Cicero discussed publishing some of his letters not long before his death, see *Letters to Atticus*, 16.5.5; White 2010, 32.

9 *Letters to Atticus*, 1.13.1; 2.19.5 and White 2010, 11-12 on those who carried letters.

10 *Letters to Atticus*, 2.9.1 Clodia Metelli is referred to as Ox-eyes; ibid, 1.14.7 mentions a Teucris who cannot be identified today.

11 *Letters to Atticus*, 2.20.3; 1.17.

12 Plutarch, *Life of Cicero*, 8.

13 For separation of property, see Crook 1990.

14 Gifts were only allowed if they did not enrich the other spouse materially (Grubbs 2002, 99-100).

15 *Letters to Atticus*, 5.9.2; 11.1.1; 11.23.1.

Rome to pay P Sallustius, possibly a relative, the same amount. And Terentia is to pay Atticus presumably from the rental income from his urban properties.[16] This role might not be particularly surprising. Due to the political nature of elite marriages, a statesman's wife would have acted as his ally, representing her husband in his absence.[17] She could visit people on his behalf or act as a go-between for those who needed to contact him. Part of this function seemed to include forwarding letters to her husband, providing the opportunity to open and read them if she so wanted.[18] He also seemed to rely on her good judgement in other respects as he entrusted important decisions to her in his absence. For instance, he asked her to find a suitable husband for their daughter and consented to her choice in advance.[19]

Second, she tried to assist him financially. A key example of this is her offer to sell some of her own property to help him during his exile, an offer that he declined.[20] Another letter refers to Tullia thanking her mother and it seems that Terentia gave her daughter money when she was in financial difficulty even though it was Cicero who should provide for her upkeep.[21] These examples are in some ways more surprising as they appear to fall outside of the expected legal behaviour of a wife. But what does that tell us? It might just show us the gap between what law dictates and how people behaved in day-to-day life. It might highlight her generosity or concern for her husband. Or perhaps she was trying to save her own skin. Once her husband went into exile, he was no longer a Roman citizen and therefore she was technically no longer his wife.[22] Legally her status was unclear and there was a serious danger that when Cicero's goods were confiscated by the state, hers would be too.[23] It appears that even if their fortunes were separate, Terentia's reputation and financial status relied somewhat on Cicero. So it was in her interest to help him.

Finally, it is also possible that she provided a third service, that of giving financial information or advice. In 49 BC, Atticus had consulted Cicero on a fi-

16 *Letters to Atticus*, 11, 11; Andreau 2001, 50.

17 For women's involvement in their husbands' political affairs, Dixon 1983; Carlon 2009, 78.

18 *Letters to Atticus*, 7.16. Cicero admitted to opening a letter of Pilia (Atticus' wife) addressed to his brother (*Letters to Atticus*, 5.11).

19 Gardner 1991, 41; Treggiari 2002, 61. It was also practical given that the fastest courier took 27 days from his province Cilicia.

20 *Letters to his Friends*, 14.1; 14.2.

21 *Letters to his Friends*, 14.6, for this interpretation, Dixon 1986, 104.

22 Lintott 2008, 179.

23 Treggiari 2007, 58-59; Dixon 1986, 96-98.

nancial matter and Cicero referred him to Terentia and Philotimus.[24] Atticus was a close friend but he was also a shrewd and successful businessman with an impressive financial and political network. Did Terentia have much financial knowledge or experience to share? It is known that Terentia was richer than Cicero and appears to have managed successfully a vast fortune.[25] It is not known if she advised Cicero himself on financial matters. Elsewhere, Atticus made a joke about bankers that Cicero did not understand but she did.[26] These letters also show us that she was privy to the contents of Atticus's letters which Cicero might have read to her.[27] Similar comments are made about Tullia enjoying Atticus' letters.[28]

There is one matter, this time spending money, where we might have expected to find Terentia's input and it is absent. Besides advising Cicero on a range of issues from politics to literature, Atticus seems to have filled another role: interior decorator. Cicero bought his Tusculan villa around 68 BC and discusses it with almost child-like glee to his friend. He expected Atticus to buy ornaments to furnish his villa trusting him on both taste and price.[29] We are left with the intriguing question of: was Terentia involved in some way in this? The surviving letters to her are unfortunately silent on this topic. Atticus' involvement could have a number of explanations. It might have been due to the separation of marital property. Or was it because he was decorating it in Greek style and Atticus, living in Greece at the time, was well placed to get what he needed? Perhaps Atticus was put in charge of helping him to decorate certain rooms (such as the Academy and library) and Terentia others.

Moral support

These examples suggest that financial matters were freely discussed between Cicero and his wife. When Cicero went into exile in 58 BC, Terentia offered to join him but he did not agree to it on the grounds that it was his burden to bear, her health was poor and that she was more useful in Rome.[30] Only four letters survive to her from this period and they show that topics shared were not only of

24 *Letters to Atticus*, 7.22.
25 While Cicero seemed to struggle financially, Terentia was able to contribute substantially to her son's upkeep: Dixon 1986, 108-110.
26 *Letters to Atticus*, 7.13; 7.13a.
27 See also the end of *Letters to Atticus*, 2.12.
28 *Letters to Atticus*, 10.13.
29 *Letters to Atticus*, 1.4; 1.5; 1.6; 1.8; 1.9; 1.10; 1.11.
30 *Letters to his Friends*, 14.3.

a practical nature such as finance, but an emotional one. It is in providing him moral support that she keeps information from Cicero.

It is important to try and appreciate what is understood of Cicero's state of mind at this time. The exile devastated him as it robbed him of everything that he had worked so hard to achieve. It has been argued that his grief during exile was little different from that he experienced at the death of his daughter.[31] In reaction he seemed to withdraw from everybody including those close to him, as evidenced in his refusal to see his brother even at the risk of causing offence which he later worked hard to repair.[32] His success and status were embodied in his house on the Palatine that was looted and burned down along with his other properties.[33] So, in addition to the physical separation from his wife, they technically no longer had a 'home' of their own which could afford some protection from outside intrusion.[34] Cicero struggled to protect his personal integrity as well as the private life of his family.[35]

After Cicero's departure, Terentia donned mourning clothes and went about with Tullia to arouse sympathy for their plight and to lobby for Cicero's reinstatement. It was a very public and humiliating action that she did tirelessly, diligently and uncomplainingly. While working for his return, his replies to her letters hint at the incredible support she was giving him. She showed concern for his safety, writes that it is not his fault and asks him to be courageous and hopeful.[36] Despite very few surviving letters to her from this period, it seems that they were in constant contact from the references to her in his letters to Atticus.[37] In response Cicero acknowledges her efforts, empathises with her hardships and thanks her.

She passed on any news to him that offered a glimmer of hope yet she also held certain information back from him fearing that it would have negative impact on his fragile state of mind. The prime example is when she was taken against her will from the Temple of Vesta to the Tabula Valeria although we do not know the exact nature of her mistreatment. Later references to this incident in his

31 Hutchinson 1998, 26.

32 *Letters to Quintus and Brutus*, 1.3, and discussion in Hutchinson 1998, 38-47.

33 Hales 2000.

34 The Roman household was not especially private by modern standards due to the presence of many slaves, see Veyne 1985 81-82. The Stoic philosopher Diodotus lived with them for many years (*Letters to Atticus*, 2.20).

35 See Solove 2008, 12-38 for these and other facets embodied in the concept of privacy.

36 *Letters to his Friends*, 14.1; 14.3; 14.4 for discussion of the latter, Hutchinson 1998, 28-33.

37 *Letters to Atticus* 3.5, 3.8, 3.9, 3.19.

speeches imply that it was both physical and verbal.[38] She must have known that he would find out eventually about it, yet it is significant that he did not hear about it from her.[39]

Did this role continue? It is more difficult to speak about moral support in the later period. Fifteen of Cicero's letters to Terentia survive from July 48 BC to October 47 BC, the period immediately after he defected from Pompey's camp. The contents show that she continued in her role as intermediary in financial matters as well as sending on letters and news from Rome.[40] These letters are brief, begin with a formula (*si vales, bene est, valeo*) and not a personalised greeting and there is a notable absence of emotional content.[41] In letter 14.6, dated to 15 July 48, he explains why he writes so seldom to her as there being little he cares to write about.[42] On the very same day, he wrote a long and detailed letter to Atticus in which he exclaims: if only I could talk to you instead of writing.[43] Perhaps these were topics that husband and wife were not accustomed to discussing? Or could the brevity of these letters be an attempt by Cicero to hold information back from her?

His letters to Atticus also seem to show a shift in the marital relationship at this time, both in their structure and their contents. Cicero tended to begin or end his letters with personal matters while important matters for discussion were developed in the middle. In the majority of the letters to Atticus before 48 BC, Terentia is mentioned only at the beginning and the end, often along with other family members. Mostly she sends her regards to Atticus or thanks him for a favour or his hospitality. At the beginning of one letter Cicero describes the arrival of Terentia and Tullia at Formiae full of news of the kindness Atticus showed them.[44] At the end of another letter Cicero tells Atticus that Terentia is suffering with rheumatism and she sends her love to Atticus and his family.[45]

But this is not the case in his letters to Atticus dating from 48 BC. Her place shifts to the middle and is sometimes masked in Greek.[46] In one letter, he begins dictating to a scribe, but then takes the pen to write himself on a confidential

38 *On his House*, 59; *Pro Sestio*, 145.

39 *Letters to his Friends*, 14.2.

40 *Letters to his Friends*, 14.6, 14.8, 14.21.

41 White 2010, 73 and Claassen 1996, 216 argue that the brevity and language can be explained by other factors than lack of affection.

42 *Letters to his Friends*, 14.6.

43 *Letters to Atticus*, 11.4.

44 *Letters to Atticus*, 7.18.

45 *Letters to Atticus*, 1.5.

46 For use of Greek in the letters, Hutchinson 1998, 13-15.

matter: Terentia and her will.[47] In another letter Cicero seems to suspect a lack of transparency in her handling of financial affairs and he appears to question her for the first time.[48]

Sometime around 46 BC Cicero divorced his wife of more than 30 years. It cost him significantly both financially as he was unable to repay the dowry and in terms of reputation.[49] The reasons are not known. Plutarch says that Terentia neglected Cicero during the civil war, did not visit him in Brundisium and implied that she was stealing from him.[50] Modern interpretations reflect similar ideas: that he became obsessed with the idea she was stealing from him; that she was unsympathetic to him during his stay in Brundisium and that she was acting dishonestly.[51]

An ideal wife?

A study of the contents of the letters has revealed two shared aspects of their married life: the financial and moral support of Terentia. What can they tell us about Cicero's ideas regarding the qualities of an ideal wife compared to those of his social peers? Cicero must have had expectations of his wife that went beyond her dowry and her political support.[52] This section will try and answer this question by looking at how he praises his wife and compare it to the praise of women in the letters of Pliny the Younger.[53] This brief comparison throws up yet another possible reason for their divorce encompassed in the idea of devotion.

In his letters to Terentia, Cicero praises her with having the following attributes: kind, diligent, courageous, virtuous, upright, faithful, generous and devoted.[54] In his speeches and in a letter to his brother he refers to Terentia's devotion

47 *Letters to Atticus*, 11.24.

48 *Letters to Atticus*, 11.16; Lintott 2008, 325 all references to her are about money.

49 Dio Cassius, *Roman History*, 46.3-4.

50 Plutarch, *Life of Cicero*, 41. Plutarch (AD 46 – c120) was a moral philosopher and ancient biographer whose work *Parallel Lives* relates the lives of many prominent Greeks and Romans.

51 Claassen 1996, 209-10.

52 Cicero translated Xenophon's *Oeconomicus* which includes advice on a wife's role in household management.

53 Of course it cannot be assumed that the concept of an ideal wife had not evolved by the time that Pliny lived. For some background, Pomeroy 1995, 149-89; Fantham et al. 1994, 294-329.

54 *Letters to his Friends*, 14.1; 14.2; 14.4.

or loyalty.[55] Pliny the Younger, who puts forward a number of women as ideal wives, uses the following qualities in praise of Clodia Fannia: sexual purity, integrity, dignity, steadfastness and devotion.[56] Memorials set up to commemorate wives illustrate that sexual purity, integrity and devotion were considered desirable qualities in wives and important in a successful marriage.[57]

One quality found on every list is *pietas* or devotion. It particularly stands out in the letters of Pliny the Younger as the defining characteristic of exceptional women. Pliny's favourite possessor of this quality was Arria, wife of Aulus Caecina Paetus, who was well known to the Romans for committing suicide with her husband when he was condemned to death by Emperor Claudius. When her husband hesitated to commit the act, she took the sword from him, thrust it into her own breast and handed it back saying: 'It doesn't hurt Paetus'.[58] Arria's granddaughter, named Fannia, followed her husband, Helvidius Priscus, twice into exile before being exiled herself. Pliny, who seemed to consider the eldest Arria as an exemplary wife, did not find her suicide to be the most praiseworthy of her actions. He tells another story of how she kept news of their son's death from her husband when her husband was critically ill so as not to further endanger his health.[59] This earlier act is the more important because it was done with no expectation of reward.[60]

It might be possible to understand Terentia's actions outlined earlier in terms of devotion. During his exile, Terentia appears to have done her utmost to assist him in his time of need. She offered to join him in exile, kept hurtful information from him, braved humiliation and risked her personal safety at the same time that she offered him both the emotional and financial support he needed. Here she seems to correspond to Pliny's and possibly Cicero's idea of a devoted wife.

Was she still devoted to him in the later period of 48-47 BC? As mentioned earlier, it appears that her financial role continues. There is little evidence of moral support in the few surviving letters but the letters are incredibly difficult to interpret. For instance, in two replies to her, both dated November 48, she had expressed the wish to visit Cicero and then to be nearer to him: he did not agree to either.[61] Is he doing this out of her best interests as before or is he pushing her away? What is apparent is a constant supply of advice and emotional support

55 *Pro Sestio*, 49; *Letters to Quintus and Brutus*, 1.3.

56 *Letters of Pliny the Younger*, 7.19. For discussion see Carlon 2009, 54 and 175-76.

57 Shelton 1990, 177-78; Carlon 2009, 164.

58 *Letters of Pliny the Younger*, 3.16; Martial 1.13.5; Tacitus, *Annals*, 16.34.

59 *Letters of Pliny the Younger*, 3.16.

60 Carlon 2009, 44.

61 *Letters to his Friends*, 14.12; 14.19.

coming from Atticus.[62] Why might she have stopped being devoted to him? Plutarch describes her as ambitious which the Romans considered a negative quality in a woman.[63] In marrying a brilliant but unknown man in Roman politics, she risked her family's fortune and reputation.[64] Up until his exile, he was on the political rise – indeed he could do little wrong.[65] Ten years later the situation had significantly changed; he had made political mistakes.[66] His reputation was no longer sure.[67] Did she lose interest in him once his star started to decline? Maybe she was disappointed in him? All of which might have made his indecisiveness and his self-pitying exaggerations difficult to bear.[68] Of course a Roman male would not have seen it this way. As Pliny shows, the devotion of Arria and Clodia Fannia to their husbands knew no limits.

This is entirely speculation and it is important not to be misled by it. If Cicero shared Pliny's high expectations regarding the devotion of a wife, and we cannot know this for sure, it is unlikely that he shared all of Pliny's views on women. The letters suggest that Cicero respected his wife in general, one example was seen with her handling of financial matters until somehow he was forced to question it. Pliny, who upheld his wife as a role model, treated her like a child and in the letters at least she is only appreciated for her contribution to his *gloria*.[69] Pliny also portrays elite women as financially illiterate and needing the protection of a male (which he is happy to provide).[70] But scholars have often questioned the extent to which Cicero shared the same ideas as his social peers. The affection and regard he expresses for his daughter Tullia and his freed slave Tiro may not have been typical.[71]

62 *Letters to Atticus* 11.5, 11.6, 11.7, 11.8 for some examples.

63 See note 6 for reference.

64 Treggiari 2007, 32.

65 For some background on his life and career, see the introduction of Shackleton Bailey's translation of the *Letters to Atticus*, 2006, 1-25.

66 He refused the post of legatio offered by Caesar (*Letters to his Friends*, 14.3); *Letters to Atticus*, 2.18. Tatum 1999, 156 argues it was not a mistake.

67 Treggiari 2007, 84.

68 Indecisive: *Letters to Atticus*, 7.14, 7.16, 7.17, 7.18, 7.23; Self-pity: ibid, 3.4, 3.8.

69 *Letters of Pliny the Younger* 8.10; Carlon 2009, 16, 165.

70 *Letters of Pliny the Younger* 2.4.

71 For Cicero's description of Tullia, *Letters to Quintus and Brutus*, 1.3; Treggiari 2002, 69-70; Carlon 2009, 52.

Conclusion

Stories about ideal wives in the form of *exempla,* which were commonly recorded by Roman writers, were important indicators of cultural norms and values. Even if some ancient writers glorified women in the domestic sphere, the *exempla* tended to highlight women who had masculine traits.[72] By necessity Cicero and Terentia worked closely together to attain the level of political success that Cicero enjoyed. For this to work it seems that Terentia not only provided him with the wealth (in the form of a dowry) and was expected to possess a number of exemplary qualities (like courage and devotion) but also needed to have an intimate knowledge of his politics, his finances and his character.

The modern reader only glimpses the real Cicero in his letters. The roles he played and the images he projected of himself varied depending on who he was writing to.[73] Any attempt at trying to paint a picture of Terentia is even more fraught with difficulty. With the distance of time, culture and language, what we know of her actions are open to too many interpretations. Often she is the one to come out looking bad.[74] At the risk of looking at her too much through modern eyes, she seems to have been a woman who managed successfully a considerable fortune as well as a highly intelligent but difficult man. She suffered from illness her entire life, survived the ups and downs of her husband's high profile career and the death of a much-loved daughter yet she comes across as generous, giving, capable, forebearing.[75] While Cicero seems to have appreciated her, perhaps she felt he did not appreciate her enough, making her less than the ideal wife.

Bibliography

Andreau, J. 2001. *Banque et affaires dans le monde romain.* Paris: Éditions du Seuil.

Carlon, J.M. 2009. *Pliny's Women: Constructing Virtue and Creating Identity in the Roman World.* Cambridge: Cambridge University Press.

Cicero, *Letters to Quintus and Brutus*. Edited by J. Henderson, translated by D.R. Shackleton Bailey, 2002. Cambridge: Harvard University Press.

Cicero, *Letters to His Friends*. Edited by T.E. Page, E. Capps, W.H.D. Rouse, L.A. Post, E.H. Warmington, translated by W.G. Williams, 1954. Cambridge: Harvard University Press.

Cicero, *Letters to Atticus*. Edited by J. Henderson, translated by D.R. Shackleton Bailey, 2006. Cambridge: Harvard University Press.

72 Parker 1998, 168-69; Carlon 2009, 185.

73 White 2010, 170.

74 Treggiari 2007, 155 n.1.

75 She lived to be 103 according to Pliny the Elder, *Natural History*, 7.158.

Cicero, *The Speeches, De Domo Sua (On his House)*. Edited by T.E. Page, E. Capps, W.H.D. Rouse, L.A. Post, E.H. Warmington, translated by N.H. Watts, 1965. Cambridge: Harvard University Press.

Cicero, *The Speeches, Pro Sestio and In Vatinium*. Edited by T.E. Page, E. Capps, W.H.D. Rouse, L.A. Post, E.H. Warmington, translated by R. Gardner, 1966. Cambridge: Harvard University Press.

Cicero, *De Officiis (On Duties)*. Edited by T.E. Page, E. Capps, W.H.D. Rouse, L.A. Post, E.H. Warmington, translated by W. Miller, 1913. Cambridge: Harvard University Press.

Claassen, J. 1996. 'Documents of a Crumbling Marriage: The case of Cicero and Terentia'. *Phoenix*, 50, 208-32.

Crook, J.A. 1990. 'His and hers: What degree of financial responsibility did husband and wife have for the matrimonial home and their life in common, in a Roman marriage?'. In J. Andreau and H. Bruhns (eds.) *Parenté et strategies familiales dans l'antiquité romaine*. Rome: Ecole française, 153-72.

Dio Cassius, *Dio's Roman History*. Edited by G.P. Goold, translated by E. Cary, 1969. Cambridge: Harvard University Press.

Dixon, S. 1983. 'A Family Business: Women's Role in Patronage and Politics at Rome 80-44 B.C.'. *Classica et Mediaevalia*, 34, 91-112.

Dixon, S. 1986. 'Family Finances: Terentia and Tullia'. In B. Rawson (ed.) *The Family in Ancient Rome: new perspectives*. Ithaca: Cornell University Press Croom Helm, 93-120.

Dixon, S. 1991. 'The Sentimental Ideal of the Roman Family'. In B. Rawson (ed.) *Marriage, Divorce and Children in Ancient Rome*. Oxford: Clarendon Press, 99-113.

Fantham, E., Foley, H.P., Kampen, N.B., Pomeroy, S.B., and Shapiro, H.A. 1994. *Women in the Classical World.* Oxford: Oxford University Press.

Gardner, J.F. 1991. *Women in Roman Law and Society*. Bloomington: Indiana University Press.

Grahame, M. 1997. 'Public and private in the Roman house: the spatial order of the Casa del Fauno'. In R. Laurence and A. Wallace-Hadrill (eds.) *Domestic Space in the Roman World: Pompeii and Beyond.* Portsmouth: JRA Supplementary Series 22, 137-64.

Grubbs, J.E. 2002. *Women and the Law in the Roman Empire*. London: Routledge.

Hales, S. 2000. 'At Home with Cicero'. *Greece and Rome*, 47, 44-55.

Hallett, J.P. 1984. *Fathers and Daughters in Roman Society*. New Jersey: Princeton University Press.

Hutchinson, G.O. 1998. *Cicero's Correspondence: A Literary Study*. Oxford: Oxford University Press.

Lintott, A. 2008. *Cicero as Evidence: A historian's companion*. Oxford: Oxford University Press.

Martial, *Epigrams*. Edited by T.E. Page, E. Capps, W.H.D. Rouse, L.A. Post, E.H. Warmington, translated by W.C.A. Ker, 1968. Cambridge: Harvard University Press.

Parker, H. 1998. 'Loyal slaves and loyal wives: the crisis of the outsider-within and Roman exemplum literature'. In S.R. Joshel and S. Murnaghan (eds.) *Women and Slaves in Greco-Roman Culture*. London: Routledge, 152-73.

Pliny the Elder, *Natural History*. Edited by G.P. Goold, translated by H. Rackham, 1967. Cambridge: Harvard University Press.

Pliny the Younger, *Letters and Panegyricus*. Edited by E.H. Warmington, translated by B. Radice, 1969. Cambridge: Harvard University Press.

Plutarch, *Lives of Demosthenes and Cicero*. Edited by G.P. Goold, translated by B. Perrin, 1949. Cambridge: Harvard University Press.

Pomeroy, S.B. 1995. *Goddesses, Whores, Wives and Slaves*. New York: Schocken Books.

Riggsby, A.M. 1997. ' "Public" and "Private" in Roman Culture: The Case of the Cubiculum'. *Journal of Roman Archaeology*, 10, 36-56.

Saxonhouse, A.W. 1992. 'Introduction – Public and Private: The Paradigm's Power'. In B. Garlick, S. Dixon and P. Allen (eds.) *Stereotypes of Women in Power Historical Perspectives and Revisionist Views*. New York: Greenwood Press, 1-9.

Shelton, J. 1990. 'Pliny the Younger and the Ideal Wife'. *Classica et Mediaevalia*, 41, 163-86.

Solove, D.J. 2008. *Understanding Privacy*. Cambridge: Harvard University Press.

Tacitus, *The Annals*. Edited by E.H. Warmington, translated by J. Jackson, 1969. Cambridge: Harvard University Press.

Tatum, W.J. 1999. *The Patrician Tribune*. London: University of North Carolina Press.

Treggiari, S. 2002. *Roman Social History*. London: Routledge.

Treggiari, S. 2007. *Terentia, Tullia and Publilia*. Abingdon: Routledge.

Veyne, P. 1985. *Histoire de la vie privée: De l'Empire romain à l'an mil*. Paris: Éditions du Seuil.

Wacks, R. 2010. *Privacy: A very short introduction*. Oxford: Oxford University Press.

White, P. 2010. *Cicero in Letters*. Oxford: Oxford University Press.

Visualising ancient privacy in the Roman house

Margherita Carucci

Abstract

In any discourse on the distinction between private and public space, the house is often described as the most typical place of the private and intimacy. In the Roman society, by contrast, the house of a wealthy man functioned as a public stage designed for the performance of important social rituals and for the self-presentation of the owner to a wide community. Given this striking contrast between our contemporary attitude toward domestic privacy and the Roman experience of domesticity, how might we approach the subject of privacy in Roman era? Could the members of the upper-class afford any form of privacy within their own houses? Or is privacy just a modern invention? In order to answer these questions and hence to gain a deeper understanding of the Romans' domestic experience, this paper analyses textual and archaeological evidence for the Roman elite house from the 1st century BC to the 3rd century AD. The study of ancient evidence is carried out within a specific theoretical framework for analysis, i.e.visuality, as a means to explore the ancient ambivalence between exposure and concealment or public and private.

A discussion on the notion, value, and meaning of privacy in ancient Roman times may seem thematically and chronologically out of place, since the concept of privacy was originated in modern times. As a matter of fact, the Latin vocabulary does not include any abstract term that can be translated into the English word 'privacy' despite the Latin root of the latter. The Latin term from which most European languages derive the word 'private' and other equivalents is the verb *privo*, 'to cause to be parted (from), to deprive or rob (of)'.

The ancient Romans used a nexus of different words derived from this root.[1] The adjective *privatus*, *-a*, *-um* encompasses two main meanings: restricted for the use of a particular person in reference to the private property; not holding public office in reference to a person having the status of an ordinary citizen. The noun *privatus*, *-i* describes a citizen who holds no public office, a man without a political or military position: in Imperial times (1st - 6th century AD)

I would like to thank Prof Charles Husband (University of Bradford, UK), my co-organiser in the symposium, from which the papers in this volume originate. Always offering encouragement and assistance throughout, he was a source of constant inspiration. I am very grateful to Kirsi Reyes, Programme Assistant at the Helsinki Collegium for Advanced Studies, for her endless support and high competence in the symposium management and organisation. I am also indebted to the Helsinki Collegium for Advanced Studies, which provided me with a splendid working environment during my three years as a Research Fellow in Humanities and has made a financial contribution to the publication of this book.

1 Glare 2011.

the word was used to signify anyone, regardless of political or military position, who did not hold the role of emperor. The adverb *privatim* means in private capacity, individually, in a private place, at home. As the Latin cognates are mainly used in reference to property and affairs of the state, there seems to be a general overlapping with our own use of the term privacy and other equivalents. However, none of the Latin words can encompass the wide range of meanings that the term privacy has today. It is this difference that defies any possible comparison between the Latin terms and the modern words. In tracing the origins of the word privacy, much stress is often put on the privative trait of the Latin cognate.[2] While the ancient term describes a state of being deprived of something, specifically of public office, which allows the full and appropriate functioning of a man, the modern word 'privacy' refers to a more positively rich and privileged condition being sought. In the search for meanings and values of ancient privacy, therefore, it is advisable to bear in mind that the comparison of the Roman thinking with our contemporary experience often ends up highlighting what ancient society was not rather than its complex realities. Nevertheless, as we can only understand others' concepts in relation to our own, the analysis of the Roman experience of privacy will be inevitably carried out with the help of modern notions.

The lack of a specific term does not necessarily mean the lack of experiences, phenomena, or ideological traditions to which that term refer. Anthropological studies on cultures rather different from our own in the developed West show that there are societies where the word 'privacy' does not exist.[3] Yet they have an idea or sense of the private as opposed to the public, because the notion refers to universal phenomena, such as political and social structures and relationships, housing and settlement patterns. Among these phenomena associated with the private is the housing that I would like to explore in the present contribution. More specifically, I will analyse the Romans' experience of domestic privacy from the late Republic to the early Empire (1st century BC – 3rd century AD) within a specific framework for analysis, i.e. visuality.

2 See, for example, Arendt 1998, 38.

3 The *Report of the Committee on Privacy* (Cmnd. 5012. H.M.S.O., 1972, Chap.6, para. 110) states: 'One could compile a list of societies, primitive and modern, that do not have and would not admire the norms of privacy accepted in Western Europe or North America. These differences do not prove, however, that there is no universal need for privacy. They suggest only that each society has its own forms of privacy, which may vary widely'.

Privacy and visuality

Scholars in different disciplines, such as legal studies, philosophy, social sciences, history, and anthropology, have attempted to give a single definition of the concept 'privacy' but none of these descriptions is able to grasp the variety of meanings that this notion evokes. We may conclude that the multi-dimensional aspect of privacy defies a common description. Nevertheless, there seems to be, in most definitions, a concept that often occurs in association with privacy: visibility. In the discourse on privacy, in fact, great emphasis is placed upon the individual's or group's capacity of exercising control over visual access to what is cherished as personal or private, whether it be information on the inner self or a specific space of restricted use. In this sense privacy is antithetical to publicity here defined as the person's choice of her exposure to the gaze of the others or the condition of being exposed. Within the specifically spatial dimension, the antithesis between private and public is reflected in the distinction between places whose restricted access limits the visibility of whom is inside (private) and places whose high degree of accessibility exposes their users to the others' gaze (public).

In any discourse on this antithesis, the house is often described as the most typical place of the private. However, the concept of the house as a separate place of retreat and of seclusion from the outside world is an elaboration of the modern society.[4] The root of this sharper distinction may be located in the transformation of production in early industrial capitalism, which removed the locus of production from home to factory. Society was then organized around two distinct spheres: the public as the world of the productive work, politics and men and the private as the world of the home, women, children and servants. Privacy and domesticity thus become two related terms but they are not necessarily interchangeable and cannot be always used as classificatory terms in any socio-historical context. In fact, this idea of privacy in close connection with domesticity is difficult to hold when applied to the elite house of the Roman society. Here, the house of a wealthy man was a locus of public activities, such as the reception of low-status clients and highly-ranked guests, business of all sorts, political dealings, leisure activities, and family ceremonies. They were all performed as social duties that played an important role in the public life of a rich man as a means of creating a network of social contacts and of reinforcing

4 Peter Saunders (1990, 311), one of the foremost British advocates of the centrality and importance of home, states that the home 'is the place where the self can be expressed outside of social roles and the individual can exert autonomy away from the coercive gaze of the employer and the state'.

his power and prestige. The elite house then functioned as a stage designed for the performance of those social rituals and for the self-presentation of the owner. The high publicness of the Roman house is attested even in the *cubiculum*, which is believed to be the most intimate space of the domestic dwelling according to our modern perceptions of domestic space. The term *cubiculum*, in fact, is often translated as 'bedroom' because of the etymology of the word, which derives from the verb *cubare* ('to recline, to lie asleep'). However, the analysis on the occurrences of the word *cubiculum* in Latin literature shows that the term was associated with a variety of activities, not just sleeping: murder and suicide, display of art, and the reception of friends.[5]

Given this striking contrast between our contemporary attitude toward domestic privacy and the Roman experience of domesticity, how might we approach the subject of privacy in the Roman era? Could the members of the upper-class afford any form of privacy within their own houses? Or is privacy just a modern invention? In order to answer these questions and hence to gain a deeper understanding of the Romans' domestic experience, two specific sources of evidence will be discussed: textual and archaeological. In fact, the analysis of selected literary passages containing references to activities and behaviour of elite men within the physical space of their houses can give a glimpse into the ancient users' perceptions of domestic privacy. On the other hand, the study of the material remains of the excavated Roman houses in terms of architectural and spatial features may highlight dynamics of visibility, accessibility, and exposure.[6]

Visuality: source of knowledge and power

Writing in the 1st century BC a history of Rome from its mythical origins to 264 BC, the Greek historian Dionysius of Halicarnassus makes an interesting comparison between Greek and Roman customs in the early times.

> [The Greeks] did not take any thought or keep an eye on what took place at home, holding that each man's house-door marked the boundary within which he was free to live as he pleased. But the Romans, throwing open the whole house and extending

5 Riggsby 1997.

6 As literary texts were written by the male members of the upper-class, who were also the owners of the richly ornamented and spacious houses recorded in the material evidence, the terms Romans or house-owners here will refer to the male elite of the Roman society, unless otherwise specified.

> the authority of the censors even to the bed-chamber, made them the overseer and guardian of everything that took place in the homes.[7]

The ancient Greek idea of the house as a place for personal autonomy is very close to our modern perception and use of domestic space. The ancient Romans, by contrast, promoted the interference of the state (here represented by the figure of the censor) into what might be termed the intimate sphere of the individual, namely personal relationships (master-slave, parents-children, and husband-wife) and religious practices (sacrifices and funerals), as Dionysius lists in the following passage. The Greek writer expresses surprise that the gaze of the Roman censors extended even into the bed-chamber. But in the Romans' view, direct visual observation of the citizens' home by a centralised authority guaranteed the perpetuation of the traditional social norms.[8]

The scrutinising gaze of the state may recall Foucault's discussion of the Panopticon, a model prison designed by Jeremy Bentham in the late 18th century.[9] It consists of cells concentrically arranged around a central tower, from which the prison authority constantly watches the inmates but cannot be seen. Here too, the promotion of specifically prescribed forms of behaviour – or the suppression of socially deviant behaviour- through the authority's scrutiny aims to strengthen 'the social forces'.[10] However, in the Panopticon the inmate is always the passive object of the authority's gaze by means of the prison's architectural arrangement which imposes an axial and asymmetrical visibility. In the Roman society, by contrast, every citizen could exercise what Foucault calls the 'disciplinary gaze' on his fellows in a mutual action of watching and being watched. This reciprocity of the gaze had a double advantage for the community and the individual. On the one hand, the individual's act of watching over the behaviour of his fellows guaranteed the reproduction of forms of behaviour and norms on which the traditional order of the community was based. On the other hand, being the object of the community's gaze was for the individual a means by which to prove the high standards of his morality and hence his right of membership to that community. In a sense, this sort of conduct is what is called in contemporary networked societies 'coveillance', which involves observation by equals and avoids the troubling implications of surveillance.[11]

---

7 Dionysius of Halicarnassus, *Roman Antiquities*, 20.13.2 (my translation).

8 Censorial activity was disrupted in the last century of the Republic (1st century BC), but it continued through the actions of the emperors, who took the title of censor. In the early 1st century AD, Augustus promoted a series of laws regulating what is today defined as the private life of the individual: marriage, procreation, adultery, and family.

9 Foucault 1977, 195-209.

10 Foucault 1977, 208.

11 Mann, Nolan, and Wellman 2003, 338.

Writing in about 30 AD, the Roman historian Velleius Paterculus reports an interesting dialogue between the politician Livius Drusus and his architect in charge of building Drusus' house on the Palatine of the Republican Rome in the early 1st century BC.[12]

> The architect promised him [Livius Drusus] that he would have built it [his house] in such a way that he would be free from observation and safe from all witnesses and that nobody could look down in it. But Livius replied: 'If you have any kind of skills, built my house so that whatever I am doing, I could be observed by everybody'.[13]

The architect's intention may bespeak a general idea of the house as a closed space where the owner exercises the power to shield himself from the scrutiny of the public community. By contrast, the reply of Livius Drusus as a man holding a public office (i.e. non *privatus*) shows a different sensibility and perception of the domestic space: the house of a public figure must act as an open stage for the owner's performance before the eyes of the community. What for a Roman man active in politics, that was important was not so much being virtuous as being seen to be virtuous,[14] because vision is inevitably linked with power: 'the more powerful the man, the more visible he is'.[15] This readiness to be seen, and hence judged, may heighten the vulnerability of the observed individual to certain risks. Livius Drusus, for example, was later murdered in the area on front of the very house[16] that he had wanted to be visibly accessible. Notwithstanding, a public figure who understands the necessity, and consequently the risk, of exposure for the sake of his reputation was still praised in later Imperial times as a person with a sense of honour and civic responsability.[17]

---

12 This passage is discussed by Wallace-Hadrill 1988, 46; Cooper 2007, 9-11; Milnor 2005, 65-6.

13 Velleius Paterculus, *History of Rome*, 2.14.3 (my translation).

14 The importance of viewing and being viewed is underscored in the Latin text by the number of the terms relating to the act of seeing: 'observation' (*conspectus*), 'witnesses' (*arbitris*), 'look down' (*despicere*), and 'observed' (*perspici*). For the relation between gaze and shame/honour in the Roman society, see Barton 2002.

15 Parker 1999, 167.

16 'in area domus suae': the Latin term *area* describes any empty space before or in a house. The passage does not specify the location of the space where Livius Drusus was killed.

17 The story told by Velleius Paterculus in the early 1st century AD is reported with a similar praising tone by the Greek historian and essayist Plutarch (*Moralia*, 800F: 'Precepts of statecraft') in the 2nd century AD.

The Livius story seems to highlight unbalanced dynamics of gaze and interplay between viewers and viewed objects. As in the Panopticon, the members of the Roman community are the active spectators who watch the individual holding public office from a position of visual authority. However, as mentioned earlier, the idea of Bentham's Panopticon creates a strong asymmetry of power through the asymmetry of gaze (the inmate is under constant gaze of the overseer with no possibility of reversing the roles). In Roman society, by contrast, the reciprocity of the gaze, whereby whoever is viewed can stare back at his viewers, unsettles the dynamics of power relations created by the gaze. As Livius' reply to his architect underlines, the architectural arrangement of the domestic spaces should favour a view inside the house from a specific and privileged point of view: the public space belonging to the whole community of a town. However, the same structural articulation of domestic spaces would have also allowed the inhabitants of the house to look outside onto the public area.

The way these dynamics of gaze are at work is particularly evident within the framework of the Roman villa, which was located outside the urban area and mainly used for leisure activities. In the early 2nd century AD, the Roman senator and writer Pliny the Younger describes two of his villas in two distinct letters: a seaside villa at Laurentum near Rome (2.17) and a countryside villa at Tusculum in Tuscany (5.6). In the description of these two villas, great emphasis is placed upon the view from within the domestic space towards the exterior: they may be the elements of the surrounding landscape (sea, woods, mountains, meadows, hills, vineyards) or the architectural details of the nearby inner spaces.[18] Unlike the town-house described in the textual sources, the architectural arrangement of the countryside- or seaside villa puts its inhabitant in the privileged position of the viewer of the world outside according to his time and needs. In the Plinian letters the image of the inhabitant appears as the active viewer who decides whether to be exposed to the external gaze by regulating the opening and closing of doors and windows that Piny often mentions in the description of his villas. However, as the scholar Michele George correctly points out, 'it is apparent that doors and shutters also provided seclusion from other members of the household'.[19] In fact, in the description of his Laurentine villa, Pliny speaks of a suite of rooms, which were his favourite.[20]

18 A similar emphasis on the view onto the surrounding landscape also occurs in two poems by Statius (45-96 AD) describing the Italian villas belonging to two of the poet's patrons. (*Silvae*, 1.3, 2.2.).

19 George 1997a, 318.

20 Pliny, *Letters*, 2.17.20-24. For a more detailed description of the Plinian suite as a place for intimacy see Carucci (forthcoming). Similarly, the Roman historian Suetonius (69-

When he retires to this suite, he feels that he is far away from his villa, as neither voice nor sound can penetrate the chambers. The use of curtains, windows, and anterooms along with its sound-proof partitions intensified the atmosphere of intimacy on both visual and acoustic level.

Pliny's need for withdrawal may suggest some parallels with the late 19th century definition of privacy as 'the right to be let alone',[21] which often occurs in the theoretical formulation of the social value of privacy. For example, Thomas Emerson declares that privacy 'is based upon premises of individualism, that the society exists to promote the worth and the dignity of the individual... The right of privacy…is essentially the right not to participate in the collective life – the right to shut out the community'[22]. This formulation of privacy is the product of a liberal society, which places a high value on the individual and his rights. In Roman culture, by contrast, the individual's life was not separated from that of his community, which shaped and gave sense to his personhood and personal dignity. In a sense the modern emphasis on the individual is a consequence of a growth of individualism, while in cultures like the Roman where an interdependent sense of the self prevails, the individual's existence is only defined by the presence (real of imaginary) of others. Pliny's habit of withdrawing for conducting his studies in his favourite suite of rooms, which are private because of their impermeability to sight and sound, seems to be dictated by the writer's need for privacy and personal space as they are intended today. However, as it emerges constantly throughout his letters, the goal of Pliny's writing is mainly directed toward his publicity and fame. Even in the seclusion of his rooms, Pliny writes with an awareness of the public audience and of the necessity of the participation of his private in the social.[23]

Spatial dynamics of visibility and concealment

The selected literary texts analysed above are a source of insight into ancient perceptions and uses of domestic spaces. But how did the architectural arrangement of those spaces help the owner put his house in easily accessible view or control the visual access from outside? In the following section, I will analyse a selected number of the excavated Roman houses in terms of planning, circulation, location, and accessibility.

---

130 AD) tells that the Emperor Augustus used to retire to a special place, if he had anything to do in solitude or without being interrupted (Suetonius, *Life of Augustus*, 72).

21 Warren and Brandeis 1890.

22 Emerson 1970, 545, 549.

23 On the interaction of Pliny with his community see Riggsby 1998.

The typical plan of the Italic elite house in the Republican times is centred upon the *atrium* (a courtyard roofed over but for a rectangular opening in the middle) around which a series of rooms are arranged. In the 2nd century BC, following the Greek example, another courtyard surrounded by colonnades, the so-called peristyle, was added at the rear of the *atrium* house.

Material evidence for the Italic house is mostly recorded in Pompeii (Italy), a small town that the eruption of the Vesuvius in 79 AD buried under the ashes until it was discovered in the late 18th century. In the House of Pansa VI.6.1[24] (Fig.1), for example, *atrium* (2) and peristyle (4) were arranged along the same axis which also included the entrance corridor 1, the *tablinum* 3 (the master's office used for receiving low-status clients and conducting business), the *triclinium* 5 (a dining room for the reception of high-status guests), and the garden 6 at the rear of the building. Anyone standing at the entrance would have been welcomed with a long sequence of views into the *atrium* with its central pool, the widely open *tablinum*, the peristyle, which was located two steps above the frontal area, the *triclinium* whose opening was conveniently located in correspondence with the spacing between the central columns of the peristyle, and finally the green area of the garden at the back. Through this symmetrical and sequential arrangement of a selected number of room-types, the viewer was given access to the 'public' area of the house and hence a clear picture of its owner as a man performing the social rites of cultivated Roman living. Notwithstanding, the central view axis did not lay the whole house open to scrutiny.[25] It directed the viewer's eye within a framework of selected spaces while denying a fully visual access to the rooms lying out of that frame. Therefore, while allowing the master to perform his social duties in high visibility, the view axis also permitted the other inhabitants of the house to continue their daily activities without coming under the scrutiny of the visitors. Free movement and invisibility of the household were also guaranteed by the special arrangement of some spaces. For example, the small corridor (7) running along the *tablinum* would have allowed the inhabitants to move from the *atrium* area to the peristyle zone without passing through the highly visible office of the master; the arrangement of a secondary entrance (8) also used as a stable in communication with the kitchen allowed the servants to use the service area without disturbing their master and his family.

24 Peterse 1985; Richardson 1988, 120-24.

25 Hales 2003, 107-22.

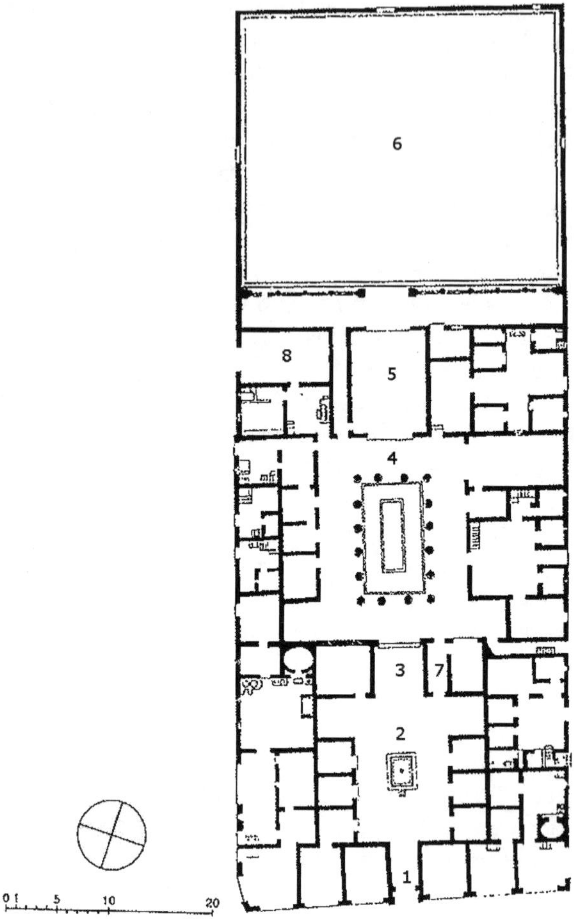

Fig.1: *Pompeii, House of Pansa: house-plan (adapted from Gros, P. 2001. L'architecture romaine du début du IIIe siècle av. J.-C. à la fin du Haut-Empire.2: Maisons, palais, villas et tombeaux. Paris: Éditions A. et J. Picard, 53, Fig. 37)*

The axial arrangement of rooms functionally important for the house-owner's publicity occurs again in a number of the so-called peristyle houses in the later Imperial times.[26]

26 The plan of these houses is dominated by the colonnaded court as the central hearth of the building and the largest unit in the entire layout with the consequent marginalisation or removal of the Italic *atrium*.

In the Maison à la Mosaïque de Vénus at Volubilis[27] (modern Morocco), for instance, a sequence of entrance area or *vestibulum* (V.1-2), peristyle (1), and *triclinium* (11) is arranged along the central axis, which guides the eyes and frames the field of vision (Fig. 2). Here too, however, specific dynamics of visibility and accessibility are at work in order to protect the inhabitants of the house from any unwanted gaze. For instance, the arrangement of the *vestibulum* three steps above the residential area increased the visibility of the lower peristyle and *triclinium*, but the viewer would have caught only a glimpse of the surrounding rooms, even if he was admitted further deep into the dining room through the courtyard. The arrangement of corridors, the separate suite of rooms around a smaller courtyard (12), and off-centre doors of the rooms opening onto the peristyle obstructed a full view of the inner parts of the rooms.

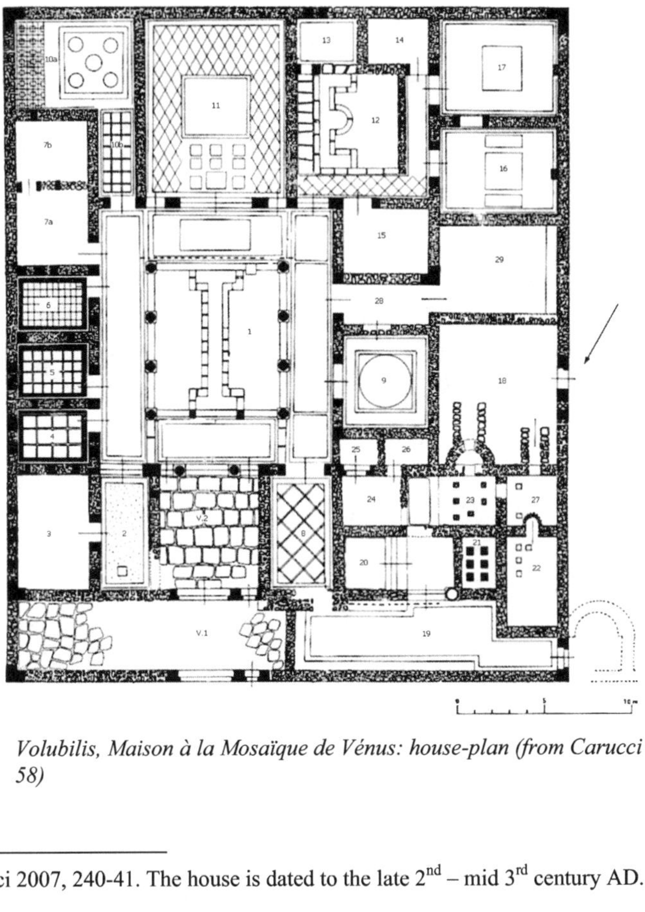

Fig.2: Volubilis, Maison à la Mosaïque de Vénus: house-plan (from Carucci 2007, Fig. 58)

27 Carucci 2007, 240-41. The house is dated to the late 2nd – mid 3rd century AD.

Similar dynamics of visibility and concealment also occur in the plan of the peristyle-houses whose main entrance is placed perpendicularly to the peristyle-*triclinium* axis.[28] In the 2nd century AD House of the Muses at Ostia,[29] near Rome, for example, the off-centre arrangement of the corridor-like *vestibulum* (1) would have allowed only a glimpse of the peristyle (2) (Fig. 3). The main door was in line with the entrance of a corridor (7) leading into two more secluded apartments (8-9) whose door openings were conveniently off-centre to secure intimacy. By contrast, the more public reception rooms (5-10-15-19) lying off the four sides of the central peristyle were in high visibility from both within and outside the rooms, since their entrance openings were in line with the openings of the columns of the courtyard. Finally, a flight of stairs (20) accessible from the *vestibulum* led to an upper floor for the possible use of the servants according to the principle of invisibility for the low-status members of the household.[30]

Archaeological evidence for the Roman house shows that, though the principle of visibility and publicity was applied to the construction of domestic spaces, the arrangement of corridors and separate suites permitted some levels of privacy or seclusion, if required. In a sense, the Roman house permitted the coexistence of visibility and privacy more than the 17th century large houses did, though both societies conceived the house as a stage where appearances mattered more than privacy. In the more modern houses, in fact, there were no corridors and each room was connected to the next so that one (family members, guests, and servants alike) had to pass through every room to get to the next.

In the Roman house, spatial articulation was employed to send visual cues establishing the power dynamics of access or seclusion within the domestic building.[31]

Further devices may have been used to make domestic spaces accessible or secluded: the presence or absence of windows and door bolts to secure a room from the inside; permeability to sight and sound; the number of people living together. But these cues are difficult to attest in the material record.

---

28 The so-called bayonette plan is attested in a number of Romano-African houses (Carucci 2006).

29 Clarke 1991, 270-88.

30 George 1997b.

31 Similar visual cues were also sent by the decoration that here is not possible to explore in detail. In general, wall-paintings and floor-mosaics illustrating figured scenes or geometric and floral patterns of complex design, which involved expenditure of time and money, were reserved for the rooms designed to receive and to entertain guests whom the house-owner wanted to impress. Decorative compositions of reduced complexity and limited colours ornamented subsidiary spaces or chambers for more personal use.

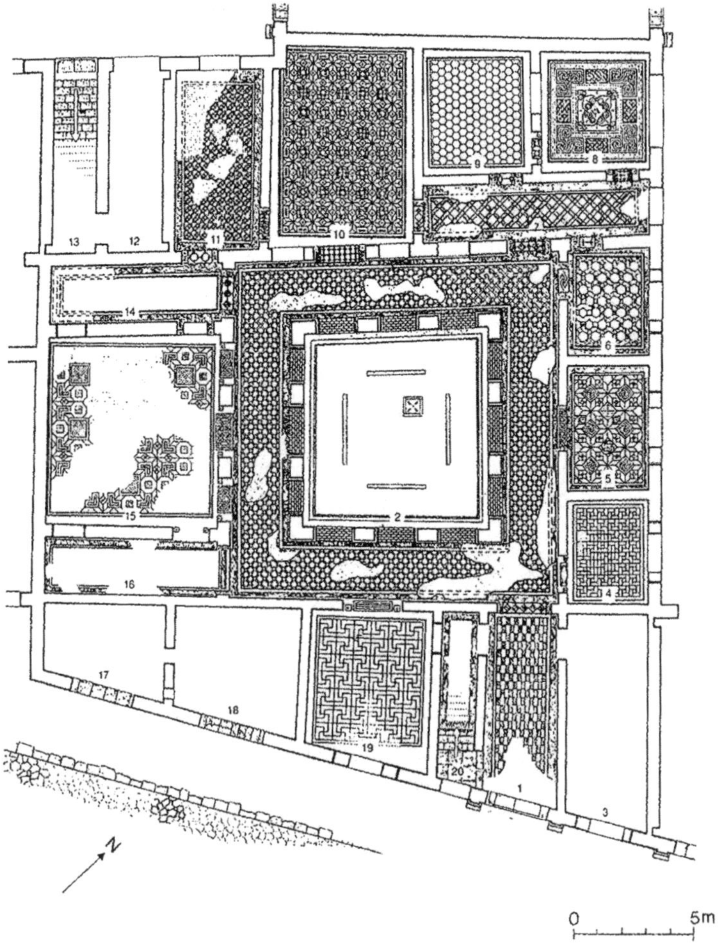

Fig.3: *Ostia, House of the Muses: house-plan (adapted from Gros, P. 2001. L'architecture romaine du début du IIIe siècle av. J.-C. à la fin du Haut-Empire.2: Maisons, palais, villas et tombeaux. Paris: Éditions A. et J. Picard, 124, Fig. 119)*

Conclusion

Archaeological evidence and Pliny's description of his villas suggest that far from the idea of the open house as emerges in the literary accounts of Dionysius of Halicarnassus and Velleius Paterculus, the Romans were concerned about the protection of what today is called domestic privacy, though on a different level.

The idea of the house as the place of the nuclear family, the growth of individualism, the removal of the servants' spaces from the master's, and the arrangement of spaces for specific activities as they occurred in the 17th century have certainly increased the value of domestic privacy. In the Roman house, by contrast, the accommodation of a larger household in the same house, the widespread presence of the servants, and the multifunctionality of the domestic space allowed a relative degree of seclusion. It is even arguable whether any wealthy Roman would have wanted a higher degree of privacy, if he had been given the choice. As said earlier, the need for publicity was deemed more important. That does not necessarily imply that moments of physical seclusion, intimacy or privacy within the domestic building were not searched for or impossible to achieve.

In lamenting the death of his friend Corellius Rufus after a long period of sickness, Pliny the Younger tells that once he went to visit his sick friend in his country house. On that occasion:

> The servants left the room; for he had this habit every time the more faithful friend entered; even his wife left, though she was very capable of keeping any secret.[32]

In a situation requiring intimacy and confidentiality, the members of the household (servants and wife) are physically removed from the room so that the individual can control the circulation of information relating to him. The control over personal information is one of the essential characteristics of privacy as it is conceptualised in modern theories. Ironically, in reporting this 'private' episode, Pliny, who mainly aims at picturing himself as an upright man whom friends can trust, ends up violating his friend Corellius' privacy by the public disclosure of previously concealed information. The publication of the letter turns out to be an important source of information for us, as it clearly shows that in the Roman society too privacy, here restricted to the dimension of control over personal information, was cherished as important, if only to foster friendship and intimacy. On some occasions, by contrast, the control over personal information may be also related to the concealment of immoral and illicit practices. The *cubiculum*, where Pliny's story is set, is also described in the textual record as the space where murders and suicides mostly take place.[33] In a society which places a high value on community evaluation, the closeness of the house to the public eye inevitably raises the suspicion that the household has something to hide. In order to overcome this ambivalence between openness and closeness or

32 Pliny, *Letters*, 1.12.7 (my translation).

33 Rigssby 1997, 39-41.

public and private, the Romans applied the principle of selective exposure, that is, the ability to control in different ways and to different extents the information one wants to bring to the attention of the public or to protect from any unwanted gaze.

Roman approach to domestic privacy certainly reveals differences from our own situation as well as similarities that allow a deeper insight into the significance of this complex notion in both ancient and contemporary societies.

Bibliography

Arendt, H. 1998. *The Human Condition*. 2nd ed. Chicago-London: University of Chicago Press.

Barton, C. 2002. 'Being in the Eyes: Shame and Sight in Ancient Rome'. In D. Fredrick (ed.) *The Roman Gaze: Vision, Power, and the Body*. Baltimore: The Johns Hopkins University Press, 216-35.

Carucci, M. 2006. 'Origins of the Romano-African House'. In J. Day, C. Greenlaw, H. Hall, A.K.L. Matassa, K. McAleese, E. Saunders and D. Stritch (eds.) *SOMA 2004 Symposium on Mediterranean Archaeology Proceedings of the eighth annual meeting of postgraduate researchers*. Oxford: BAR International Series, 17-23.

Carucci, M. 2007. *The Romano-African domus: studies in space, decoration, and function*. Oxford: BAR International Series.

Carucci, M. forthcoming. 'Intimacy in the *Cubiculum*: From Textual Sources to Material Evidence in Roman Africa and Iberia'. In A. Anguissola (ed.) *Privata Luxuria: Towards an Archaeology of Intimacy*. Munich: Utz Verlag.

Cooper, K. 2007. 'Closely Watched Households: Visibility, Exposure and Private Power in the Roman Domus'. *Past & Present*, 197, 3-33.

Emerson, T. I. 1970. *The system of freedom of expression*. New York: Random House.

Foucault, M. 1977. *Discipline and punish: the birth of the prison*. Translated from the French by Alan Sheridan. London: Allen Lane.

George, M. 1997a. 'Repopulating the Roman House'. In B. Rawson and P. Weaver (eds.) *The Roman Family in Italy: Status, Sentiment, Space*. Oxford: Clarendon Press, 299-319.

George, M. 1997b. 'Servus and Domus: the Slave in the Roman House'. In R. Laurence and A. Wallace-Hadrill (eds.) *Domestic Space in the Roman World: Pompeii and beyond*. JRA, Suppl. Ser., 22, Portsmouth, 15-24.

Glare, P. G. W. (ed.), 2011. *Oxford Latin dictionary*. 2nd ed. Oxford: Oxford University Press.

Hales, S. 2003. *The Roman House and Social Identity*. Cambridge: Cambridge University Press.

Mann, S., Nolan, J. and Wellman, B. 2003. 'Sousveillance: Inventing and Using Wearable Computing Devices for Data Collection in Surveillance Environments'. *Surveillance & Society*, 1.3, 331-55.

Milnor, K. 2005. *Gender, domesticity, and the age of Augustus: inventing private life*. Oxford: Oxford University Press.

Parker, H.N. 1999. 'The Observed of All Observers: Spectacle, Applause, and Cultural Poetics in the Roman Theatre Audience'. In: B. Bergmann and C. Kondoleon (eds.) *The Art of Ancient Spectacle*. New Haven and London: Yale University Press, 162-79.

Peterse, K. 1985. 'Notes on the Design of the House of Pansa (VI.6.1) in Pompeii'. *Mededelingen van het Nederlands Instituut te Rome*, 46, 35-56.

Richardson, L. 1988. *Pompeii: an architectural history*. Baltimore-London: Johns Hopkins University Press.

Riggsby, A. M. 1997. ' "Public" and "Private" in Roman Culture: the Case of the Cubiculum'. *Journal of Roman Archaeology*, 10, 36-56.

Riggsby, A. M. 1998. 'Self and Community in the Younger Pliny'. *Arethusa*, 31.1, 75-97.

Rybczynski, W. 1986. *Home: a short history of an idea*. New York: Viking.

Saunder, P. 1990. *A Nation of Home Owners*. London: Unwin Hyman.

Wallace-Hadrill, A. 1988. 'The Social Structure of the Roman House'. *Papers of the British School at Rome*, 56, 43-97.

Warren, S. D. and Brandeis, L. D. 1890. 'The Right to Privacy'. *Harvard Law Review*, 4.5, 193-220.

Multiple privacies: Nesting spheres of intimacy in Western Siberian indigenous lifestyles

Elena Liarskaia and Stephan Dudeck

Abstract

Anthropological fieldwork in two indigenous communities in Western Siberia leads us to this paper. During our fieldwork with Nenets and Khanty reindeer herders we came across incidences that reveal an understanding of privacy and intimacy that differs from the concepts of mainstream society. The borders around a person that prevent the flow of information and interaction establish a sphere we call intimacy and secure the integrity of the person; they define the culturally specific perceptions of personhood. Anthropology can thus help us to understand that notions of privacy or intimacy are not defined by the content of information which is kept private. They describe culturally different ways of drawing borders around certain knowledge. We believe that the fieldwork method of participant observation used by anthropologists is a unique way to reveal these differences.

Borders of privacy and intimacy are not only drawn around the individual person but they are also able to embrace different collectives in nested relations and fractal recursion, as Susan Gal has shown.[1] Anthropological research experiences a major methodological challenge in exploring these spheres of cultural intimacy.[2] We will draw upon examples from our anthropological fieldwork with Nenets and Khanty[3] reindeer herders in two indigenous communities in Western Siberia to demonstrate that concepts of privacy are not stable and differ not only between societies but inside societies between social groups defined by status, age, and gender of their members. Inside the communities these concepts are connected to perceptions of purity and impurity[4] or to taboo practices like the Khanty 'yimelta'. Gender and kinship relations or the concept of body, clothing, and housing are connected here with the

We must gratefully note the support of the Max-Planck Institute for Social Anthropology, Halle/Saale, Germany and the Finnish Academy ORHELIA project, funding decision 251111 of 2011. We would like to express our gratitude to our colleagues in the Siberian Studies Centre of the Max-Planck Institute for Social Anthropology for their useful comments and discussion.

1 Gal 2005.

2 cf. Herzfeld 2000.

3 Nenets are nomadic reindeer herders in the tundra zone, Khanty are half nomadic hunters, fishermen and reindeer herders in the taiga zone of Western Siberia. Both communities had to cope with the influx of Russian speaking population since the Russian colonisation 400 years ago and with rapid population grow and urbanisation since the 1960s due to oil and gas development.

4 cf. Лярская 2005.

cosmological order - the relation of different beings embedded in the order of space and time. Relations to settler communities as well as to the deceased, to the animal world, and the supernatural beings are part of the nesting privacies that include avoidance and hiding and the distinction between official and unofficial spheres. It is important to acknowledge that these borders are not given but always enacted and performed: they change during the lifecycle of the person as well as due to historical transformations. Georg Simmel made the important point in connection to privacy that what is of primary importance is not the information contained but the practices of keeping the secrets that are part of interaction and social connectedness.[5] They determine the respect, dignity, and the social face of persons and collectives in a given context.

Conflicting notions of private spheres

A Khanty woman living on a nomad camp in the forest complained:

> 'Russian men do not know how to behave in the forest. They think they are alone here. They are drinking and spitting and relieve themselves wherever they want. In our houses they are behaving as if there were no women or children around and use offensive language. Russian men do not understand that the forest is our home. Everything has its place here.'

For these Russian men, the woman is speaking about, the forest is an exclusively male place designated for recreation practices like hunting and partying. Alcohol and transgressive behaviour are markers of a private and informal atmosphere. From the perspective of the indigenous Khanty, on the contrary, the forest is a much more public space where different categories of beings have to meet each other with respect. There are animals and spirits, sacred places and burial grounds to be respected and the obligation of different gender and age groups to behave decently. On the other hand the forest around Khanty settlements is an intimate Khanty space guarded by the family of reindeer herders. It is not the unstructured space of uninhabited wilderness. The space in the forest is divided into profane and sacred places, female and male, directions to the underworld and the heavenly sphere and there exist clear rules of behaviour linked to that order. From the perspective of Khanty society the forest is a sphere where different beings meet and interact respectfully. In that way the forest becomes a public sphere inside the Khanty community but private in the relation to the overarching mainstream society. Russian hunters with their behaviour, which is inappropriate from the Khanty perspective, have an ambivalent position in the

5 Simmel 1908.

Khanty forest. On the one hand they represent a hegemonic concept according to which Siberian wilderness is a place outside public scrutiny. On the other hand they are often part of informal exchange networks on which Khanty reindeer herders are relying in their everyday struggle for survival.

This example already presents some of the aspects that we would like to develop further in the following paper. Firstly, notions of privacy are contested and conflicts arose around them. Secondly, different social groups have different notions about what is to be considered public and what private. And thirdly, private spheres are nesting in each other. The Khanty forest space as a place of cultural intimacy, to use a notion of Michael Herzfeld,[6] is a kind of internal public containing a number of private spheres.

Introduction to the field

Before we develop these ideas further, we want to provide an introduction into our field site in Western Siberia and its recent history.

The Khanty, Mansi and Nenets people leading a nomadic or semi nomadic life as reindeer herders, fishers and hunters traditionally inhabit the Western Siberian plain. Beginning with the 16th century they were integrated into the Russian empire. The conquest was followed by the Christianisation and the establishment of Russian trade networks. The Siberians had to deliver furs as a tax called 'yasak' to the treasury of the Tsar. In spite of the contacts with the Russians the internal social structures and traditional religious practices of the indigenous people remained relatively untouched. Contacts with the outside world were often restricted to the annual fairs where trades were made, taxes paid, children baptised, and marriages consecrated.

In the 20th century the introduction of the new Soviet order repeated the three steps of integration: the political, the ideological and the economical. After the establishment of Soviet rule shamans and local leaders called kulaks were persecuted, the local economy was organised in collective farms, and nomads were forced to get settled. In the case of the Khanty and the Nenets these attempts were much more unsuccessful than in most other regions of the Russian North. But an obligatory formal school education and health care were introduced and the Western Siberian societies changed severely with the immigration of a great number of settlers after the Second World War and especially since the 1960s with the development of large oil and gas deposits.

6 Herzfeld 2000.

The indigenous population now makes up less than 5% of the region's population. Nevertheless the taiga and tundra outside the towns and oil and gas fields remain almost exclusively the domain of the indigenous reindeer herders.

Research question

During our ethnographic field-research we repeatedly had to deal with conflicting notions of privacy and intimacy and collected material linked to informational borders around persons and collectives. The following considerations are an attempt to transform an unsystematic collection of incidents that seemed not linked to each other into material for analysis. Our method of participant observation has to deal with a special kind of material belonging to areas of so called cultural intimacy which are usually excluded from public representation and often associated with emotions like shame and embarrassment. Obviously these emotions are linked to different practices in different cultural contexts and these differences became the starting point for our endeavour.

The Western idea of intimacy evolves out of a concept of the person as a singular autonomous self bound by a physical body and inhabited by an independent mind. As French anthropologist Marcel Mauss[7] had shown already in the 1930s, this concept of the person is an ideal derived from Roman law, Stoa philosophy, and Christian theology but prevailed only in modern times. Non-European concepts of the self were presented by Mauss as alternative but evolutionary lower forms of the concept of the autonomous individual. These alternative models of personhood and related concepts of the private are often presented as some radical other to the Western European ideal. One example is the concept of so-called Soviet split consciousness: Soviet citizens had to learn to switch between the moral orders of everyday life and official ideology. Public speech and private everyday practice often followed contradictory ideals. The distinction between the private and the public was situational and not as fixed to spatial structures as in the Anglo-Saxon world.[8] According to authors like Alexei Yurchak[9] or Susan Gal[10] one does not need the concept of split consciousness to distinguish between these situations. The presence of official institutions and their representatives and the use of specific language markers characterise public and official situations. Informality is marked by other forms

7 Mauss 1979.
8 cf. Gal 2005.
9 Yurchak 2003.
10 Gal 2005.

of communication: the appearance of alcohol, for instance, can mark the switch of a situation from being official to becoming informal without any change of people or space.

To be able to grasp the whole variety of concepts of privacy and intimacy we start with a broad outline of the field of privacy without distinguishing between the private, the intimate, the personal, etc., or giving precise definitions of the content of these concepts.

We use the term private and intimate here in a broad sense for the different spheres that surround a person and face-to-face collectives in a given cultural context. They are spheres that enclose verbal information as well as visible or audible knowledge that should remain exclusive for situations, spaces and groups of people. We are interested in the practices that are connected to the borders of these spheres, to their transgression, violation, and change. We believe that people have ideas about what should remain inside and outside these borders and clear concepts about the appropriate content of the intimate and the private. But they also have collectively shaped norms how the transgression and change of these borders should or should not proceed. These norms are guided and guarded by emotions like shame and embarrassment as well as excitement, pleasure, and satisfaction. To use the theatrical metaphor of Erving Goffman,[11] private spheres are backstage regions in relation to the public arena: they are spheres where the public image is produced for its public performance.

Examples

There is no exact translation of the word 'privacy' in Khanty or Nenets language, but there is a terminology for the practices connected to the borders of the individual. We have no reason to believe that in these societies the person, who has a concept of his own grammatical 'I', his physical and social face, his body and place in the kinship network, does not have any imagination of himself as an individual person. Individuality and independence are on the contrary a highly valued character trait in these nomadic cultures. But we assume that the way the individual person relates to others in these indigenous communities is built upon different principles than that of the modern Western concept of the person.[12] We will present in the following some native practices and concepts of the demarcation of the borders of what can be called intimacy or privacy.

11 Goffman 1959.

12 Actually there is no reason to believe that there exists only one clearly defined concept of the self and the individual person in Western societies or the (sub-) cultural variety of practices connected to privacy and intimacy could be reduced to such a single concept.

One of the most visible practices of this kind in everyday life is the veiling of the Khanty women's faces by a headscarf. The concept behind this practice, which consists of rules to avoid interaction, first of all with older relatives of the patrilineage of one's spouse, is called ʻyimilta' in Khanty language. The face of one's wife has to stay invisible to the father and all elder brothers of the husband. But avoidance is not restricted to women. The son in law has to observe a certain avoiding attitude in the presence of his father in law and older relatives of the patrilineage of his wife. Practices connected to *yimilta*, such as the hiding of a person behind a headscarf or behind a curtain, encompass first of all visibility, but they also contain other forms of communication, such as the verbal, i.e. the avoidance of direct addressing and speech. The *yimilta* rules include the avoidance of knowledge of practices that are linked with the body of a person, like relieving oneself, washing, and sexual intercourse. Veiling practices were the most provocative cultural trait to the early Soviet attempts to integrate the Khanty people into Soviet society. Serious conflicts arose when the Soviet authorities tried to put a halt to the practice of veiling with the headscarf, as it was considered a symbol of the lower social status of women. Contrary to the intended effect, women experienced the unveiling not as an act of emancipation but as degrading and humiliating. Not only was their feeling of intimacy violated but they were also deprived of the possibility to show respect to their relatives. As a reaction they pursued to wear the headscarf in uncontrolled spaces. When persecution diminished later, they again started to wear it publicly. Today one can even see Khanty women wearing their headscarf in the villages and towns. The custom of hiding the face even became a sign of the reindeer herders' identity in contrast to the Russified villagers.

Contrary to popular belief, the *yimilta* rules do not separate genders but regulate the relationship of patrilineages connected by marriage. They are not given but have to be introduced during the marriage in specific rituals, which do not necessarily include only the rules of avoiding. There also exist rituals with the purpose of removing certain *yimilta* rules. This happens, for instance, when older people marry and the veiling of the face in the presence of people who have already seen them during their whole life does not make sense. Our field material contains instances where elders allowed a forbidden behaviour in certain instances through a small ritual.

The above described avoidance relationship (*yimilta*) to certain relatives in different patrilineages has its reverse counterpart in certain other types of relationships between other relatives that have especially close and immediate relations. These are for instance the relationship between the younger brother of the mother and his nephew or niece, or the relationship between the husbands of sisters. These are relatives that also belong to different patrilineages according to the Khanty kinship system. It is also important to remark that the rules of avoiding do not alienate people from each other. The daughter-in-law usually lives together with her parents-in-law in the same household and shares all everyday things with them.

Matryoshka

Another principle organising communication and interactional borders is linked to the human body. For example, in Nenets and Khanty cultures the back of a person is considered of especially spiritual importance; the clothing is linked to the status of the person and subjected to similar regulations of treatment: worn clothing is not treated as waste but deposited at special places in the forest. The same principle is extended to the house or tent: the back-wall is considered as the sacred backbone of the building so that crossing behind the house is considered as a violation of its integrity and the religious status of the host. The geographical order of the surrounding landscape, containing sacred places, settlements, hunting grounds, and cemeteries is a further extension linked to the body of the patrilineage with its backbone and head to the north and its extremities to the south. In that way space is organised like a matryoshka doll with spheres nesting into each other and formed by the same principle.

Dichotomies

Internal borders of information and interaction are organised along dichotomies that sometimes resemble each other but more often cross each other like age and gender. Above we already wrote about the division into patrilineages with a common patrilineal ancestor and the rules of *yimilta* that are also connected to age and gender differences. The interaction across other dichotomies are organised in a similar way. These are the relationships of the living with the dead, of the older generation with the younger one, of the Khanty community and their shamans with the gods, of the hunters to the game (especially the most important and sacred one, the bear), and finally the relationship between reindeer herders and authorities - the state and the oil companies.

The restrictions follow the same rules described above. So did we experience, for instance, the avoidance of visibility between the elder generation and the younger one, when the researcher incidentally showed pictures of youngsters partying to their elder relatives. The parents know what their offspring is doing but it is not respectful to let parents see their children's transgressive behaviour. In a similar way in the Nenets culture conjugal infidelity is certainly considered very bad, but it is considered much worse if the unfaithful one did not manage to hide his or her behaviour, or his or her partner got to know about his or her unfaithfulness. This kind of behaviour is regarded as a form of total disrespect for the spouse. In many other cases it is not the information that should be kept private but the way of delivery of the information that is important to keep secret.

In the spheres of religious practices as well as hunting, or in connection to the deceased, there exists a complicated taboo language to avoid direct speech. Khanty and Nenets folklore knows, especially when it comes to sacred themes, a plethora of parallelisms and metaphors. Interaction between genders is organised horizontally according to the ritual association of the female with the earth and the underworld and the male with the heavenly gods. So it is considered dangerous if women (Khanty or Nenets) step over hunting instruments or the legs of men. As Nenets explain, women in childbearing age are the source of a certain impurity – 'syamey'. If the source of *syamey* is located above a pure being or thing, this becomes also *syamey* (impure). A contaminated person becomes ill and a contaminated thing is threatening the person who uses it. There exists a plurality of practices that regulate the behaviour of men as well as women to prevent contamination with impurity. All these rules are observed only inside the Khanty and Nenets community and mostly kept hidden from outsiders. In that way they construct a para-order that is partially veiled.

One reason for the hiding of the informal, internal and traditional rules is the contradiction to the official state jurisdiction.[13] So are for instance law on land rights and inheritance law in some cases contrary to Khanty customary law,[14] which is based on the principle that access to land and resources, property, and children have to remain inside the patrilineage the family belongs to, if Khanty elders do not decide otherwise. There exist complex Khanty rules of customary law to regulate the division of property in the case of divorce that do not comply with state law. Secrecy about the rules of the para-order strengthens the group and secures resources like internal social prestige, solidarity and participation in informal exchange networks.

All these principles of restriction are connected to the ways of interaction. Gaze and words are considered as effective and powerful as physical action is, they have performative and transformative power. Certain parts of the body, such as face, sensory organs, and the sexual organs, are especially important, as they act as the interfaces of communication.

---

13 In the concrete case this means Russian legislation.

14 Extensive information about legal pluralism and the relationship of state and customary law in Siberia can be found in the writings of N. Novikova, cf. Новикова 2002, 2003.

Analysis

After giving some examples, we will try to summarise some conclusions we could draw from them. Obviously the public spheres around the person are constructed in different ways in different cultures. Not only differ the situations linked with feelings like shame and embarrassment and the content of practices that occur in these contexts, but also the order of these situations and the stability, permeability and variability of the borders are differently constructed. We think it is useful to distinguish between the characteristics and the pragmatics of the construction of boundaries of the private.

Characteristics of the borders that surround different and nesting spheres of the private and the intimate

These borders are:

- performative: borders are produced through the practices connected to them. They are not given, but enacted, incorporated through their practice and habitualised;
- negotiated and contested: borders are not given but need special procedures like rituals to be established. There often exist special procedures of violation of the borders to demonstrate power or to subordinate others. Other procedures deal with their violation in order to restore the borders like rituals of satisfaction.[15] Traditional borders of privacy are contested for educational and medical purposes if, e.g. the doctor gains access to information or body parts that are usually kept private;
- linked to conventions: the borders respond to a system of prescriptions. They are passed down for instance as a traditional kinship terminology containing a system of social obligations;
- nested into each other like concentric spheres by repeated principles, like matryoshka-dolls;
- guarded by emotions like shame, annoyance, embarrassment and explicit rules of politeness, courtesy, moral, taboos, and rituals. The shame produced by violations of the borders of intimacy marks a damage of the reputation, the credit and finally the agency of a person. Agency is here linked to the autonomy in internal affairs like, for example, women's issues.[16]

---

15 Rituals of satisfaction are, for example, the duel or other ritual forms of taking vengeance or receiving compensation.

16 These are all affairs that are linked to the childbearing ability of women and to menstruation.

An interesting question is which kind of borders and spheres are more and which are less emotionally charged and how negative emotions are linked with positive ones - shame with lust and fear with excitement. Often these dual poles are only at nuances from each other, or follow each other in emotional ambivalent situations linked with the violation or transgression of the borders of intimacy or privacy. It would exceed the frame of our investigation to further explore these psychological problems.

Pragmatics of the borders

Here we try to systematise the practices that are connected with borders. These practices establish, transgress and transform borders often in ritual form, e.g. marriage, death, courting, etc.

People are not born within fixed borders but learn the conventions of privacy through different forms of socialisation and education which results in a modification of these borders during their lifetime. The psychological mechanisms for the maintenance of borders might not differ much from the ones in other cultures, but situations and places where the emotions occur are different according to the different constructions of the borders of intimacy.

Sometimes the borders of privacy are publicly discussed and openly reflected. In some other cases speaking and reflecting upon them has no practical reason or is highly tabooed. In the last cases the borders themselves remain invisible unless a violation occurs.

Practices of demarcation:

- performing them:
  - respecting them (reflected or unreflected, conscious or unconscious);
  - transgressing them ritually: certain norms regulate the respectful crossing of the threshold of the private and the intimate. Crossing is not automatically violating, a respectful flirt is distinct from harassment and violent intrusion in a private home distinct from a guests entering. Often these forms of regulated transgression are bound by ritual behaviour, which produces certain practices. The rules describe how, why, when, and by whom the borders can be respectfully crossed. Ignoring these rules and norms is considered violence and produces negative emotions and often causes status loss (loss of reputation, honour, etc.). Often, however, special procedures exist to restore the norms and compensate for loss of status, sometimes with reciprocal violence, like in duels, suicides or honour killings;

 – destroying them, disrespecting them, violating them.

- discussing them (discursive practices - reflecting upon them, reacting on their violations):
  – speaking about them (often in metaphorical ways);
  – punishing transgression;
  – hiding their transgression.

Our reflections on the character of the borders that mark different nesting spheres of privacy allow us to criticise concepts that are conventionally connected to the definition of the private. The first common notion of privacy is that private spheres are defined by their content (information, emotions, etc.). In opposition to the content oriented definitions, we emphasise the communicative function of the information border. It is the restriction of access to spaces, knowledge and practices, which characterise the spheres of privacy, which separate insiders and outsiders and define the way the one can become the other. A second conventional concept is that private spaces are confined spaces with clearly defined boundaries. We would rather stress the permeability of these borders: the transgression of the border is sometimes necessary for its maintenance. The flow of information and knowledge across the borders of secrecy, privacy and intimacy is necessary for the maintenance of the multiplicity of differentiated nested internal communication spaces that surround people and collectives in the societies under study. In our case all the internal Khanty concepts and practices are private issues hidden in the forest from the gaze of the mainstream society and the control of the state. They belong to the realm of the informal sphere[17] in Russia, including, for instance, criminal Mafia organisations and urban music subcultures that evolved in post-Soviet society out of the Soviet legacy of the separation of official state ideology and informal everyday practices. A third common notion is that privacy in its Western form is based on individual autonomous self-realisation. We rather argue in favour of a variety of constructions of the intimate spheres around the person and face-to-face communities even in non-European contexts. They are hidden behind a façade of the public ideal and juridical notion of the private sphere.[18] A multiplicity of notions of what belongs to the private and what should be considered intimate or what should stay secret and how these spheres are

17 The term informal is used here not only to label informal economic activities but also to describe a wide range of practices that lie outside the regulation and control of state institutions.

18 We cannot elaborate here further on the fact that the modern Western idea of privacy is linked to the emergence of the bourgeoisie as the dominant social class in European history and to the ideals of the life of the bourgeois family.

constructed, emerged not just in post-modern times or as a kind of moral plurality after the sexual revolution in the West. Socially and culturally distinct groups, often marginalised, religious communities, different forms of subcultures, secret societies, elites as well as outcasts - they all resisted a unified notion of the private, also in pre-modern times and in non-European societies.

Methodological conclusions

An important question will be how the distinct concepts of privacy could be observed and documented. Social research is difficult if the borders of intimacy are internalised and their public discussion tabooed. Only if the researcher gets to know where the borders are, she or he can analyse their configuration and what they contain. The only way to do so is to become partly integrated into the collectives under study. The researcher has to acquire and interpret the forms of metaphorical language, of joking and taboo expressions. Intimate spheres of the opposite gender of the researcher are often inaccessible or only accessible with great difficulties. There are situations, however, when certain borders become visible, often only for a short time. The ethnographic research practices to detect culturally distinct concepts of privacy could be classified in the following way:

- Observation of intercultural difference:
  - comparison of the researchers' own cultural background to that of her or his informants;
  - differences that are discussed in interethnic relations, e.g. Nenets speaking about Khanty and Russians and vice versa.

- Observation of acts of transgression:
  - documentation of involuntary transgressions by the ethnographer herself or himself;[19]
  - observation of practises in rituals of transgression;
  - observation of acts of punishment and their discussion;
  - documentation of stories about crimes or offensive, indecent behaviour.

- Observation of practices of learning during status change:
  - observation of explicit knowledge acquisition during the act/rite of passage itself;

19 See Berger 2009 and his concept of "Key Emotional Episodes" in the methodology of ethnographic fieldwork.

– documentation of knowledge acquisition through stories that teach adequate behaviour (anecdotes, gossip, tales and myth that serve as material to teach how to behave or misbehave in a certain role, when getting a certain status).

Conclusion

We believe that examples driven from anthropological fieldwork can help us to put into question conventional concepts of the private – public dichotomy. Looking at culturally specific information management we discovered organising principles to construct and maintain internal and intimate spheres and the boundaries around them that are nesting into each other. The only way to reveal these different practises of drawing borders and keeping privacy seems to be the anthropological research method of participant observation. Personal interaction and immersion of the researcher in the practises associated with the borders around the person and collectives, with the relationship between man and other beings and between social groups, is the only way to discover them. Social realities in non-European societies also help us to see differences of practices associated with the notion of privacy in 'Western' societies and to criticize essentialist notions of 'the private' and 'the public'. They can help us to overcome the common notion that the private is defined by the content of the private sphere and to understand that the practices of information management, privacy and secrecy are linked to cultural differences and borders of collectives inside the society. Understanding privacy in this way demands new ways of exploring the field of privacy. The aim of our paper is thus to present some initial thoughts on what results the methodology of an ethnographic research of the notion of privacy and intimacy could provide.

Bibliography

Berger, P. 2009. 'Assessing the relevance and effects of 'Key Emotional Episodes' for the fieldwork process'. In P. Berger (ed.) *Feldforschung: ethnologische Zugänge zu sozialen Wirklichkeiten = Fieldwork: social realities in anthropological perspectives*. Berlin: Weißensee-Verlag, 149-76.

Gal, S. 2005. 'Language Ideologies Compared: Metaphors of Public/Private'. *Journal of Linguistic Anthropology*, 15, 23-37.

Goffman, E. 1959. *The Presentation of Self in Everyday Life*. New York: Doubleday.

Herzfeld, M. 2000. 'Intimations from an Uncertain Place'. In H. G. De Soto and N. Dudwick (eds.) *Fieldwork dilemmas: anthropologists in postsocialist states*. Madison, Wis.: University of Wisconsin Press, 219-38.

Mauss, M. 1979. ‘The physical effect on the individual of the idea of death suggested by the collectivity’. In M. Mauss, *Sociology and psychology: Essays*. London: Routledge & Kegan Paul, 35-56.

Simmel, G. 1908. ‘Das Geheimnis und die geheime Gesellschaft’. In *Soziologie. Untersuchungen über die Formen der Vergesellschaftung* (1st edition). Berlin: Duncker & Humblot Verlag, 256-304.

Yurchak, A. 2003. ‘Soviet hegemony of form: everything was forever, until it was no more’. *Comparative Studies in Society and History*, 45 (03), 480–510.

Лярская, Е. В. 2005. ‘Женские запреты и комплекс представлений о нечистоте у ненцев’. *Антропологический форум. СПб*, 2, 317–26.

Новикова, Н. И. 2002. ‘Обычное право коренных народов Севера в системе российского законодательства’. In В. А. Тишков, and Н. И. Новикова (eds.) *Обычай и закон. Исследования по юридической антропологии*. Санкт-Петербург - Пушкин: Издательский дом „Стратегия‘, 175–90.

Новикова, Н. И.,2003. ‘Правовые обычаи коренных народов Севера: Кто напишет правила для оленеводов?’ In Н. И. Новикова (ed.) *Олень всегда прав: Исследования по юридической антропологии*. Москва: Издательский дом „Стратегия‘, 125–39.

Sociological and philosophical insight into privacy in postmodern cities

Karol Kurnicki and Katarzyna Salamon

Abstract

The article gives historical and philosophical insight into privacy as a deep way of understanding this phenomenon in postmodern times. By combining philosophical and sociological approaches we intend to show how privacy could be seen as one of the central issues of changing postmodern urban life. The paper focuses on the basic relationship in which the problem of privacy is entangled. We examine the issue of privacy in the context of relations present in contemporary cities and urban environment. The postmodern city might serve as a prime example of a social and physical space in which different processes concerning the individual and the society result in new forms of privacy. Changing social space of today's urban environment forces us to rethink the individual and the private space which is being negotiated by all of us in relation not only with the other, but also with the new urban environment (saturated with new media, intertextual, commodified, etc.). Changes and negotiations are directly connected with the concept of postmodern identity, which in turn relates to the historical understanding of privacy in philosophy.

In the urban space there has been always a 'battle' between what is private and what is public, since privacy and the public sphere have been defined in various ways. In a postmodern urban reality there seems to be no boundary between the private and the public spheres of activity, which also prevents the implementation of both of these dimensions of individual life. There follows a confusion of the two spaces: the private space is extensively infiltrated by the public sphere, and the public is either impossible to reach or socially and politically ineffective. Therefore, the concept and the fact of privacy have different characteristics, which are more individual and more problematic. The privacy is negotiated mainly in relation to commodities. In order to analyze the concept and the fact of postmodern privacy, we should look at its philosophical and historical origins. By identifying various philosophical views on the issues of the individual and social character of individual life, it will be possible to place the issue of privacy and the public as the two dimensions that constitute the individual life. A brief historical overview of the issues relating to the public and private contexts of the urban life in the second part will enable us to locate the processes in which city-dwellers participate. Finally, the characteristics of certain phenomena associated with today's urban reality will allow us to refer to the contradictory and unclear boundary between the categories of the private and the public in the postmodern city as well as some consequences of the status quo. Although the term 'privacy' is unclear, understood differently depending on its axiological, political or legal consequences, we can recall the distinction proposed by Bennett on the three major dimensions of privacy: individualistic, political, and instrumental.[1] We will rely mainly on two dimensions, individualistic and political, because they combine both the philosophical definition of privacy issues (individualistic) as well as the concept of public space (political). We will also describe the private and the public not as two dimensions in clear opposition to each other, as they often appear in the context of philosophical reflection or in the analysis of cities and urban change. We will rather try to describe the blurring boundary between the private and the public, as Schoeman did in his analysis on privacy in relation with social freedom.[2]

Privacy in philosophy

Is the city good for the individual? Are individual communities appropriate places for individual development and fulfilment? Such issues have always been considered by the philosophers. The individual is the inhabitant of two worlds: the world of nature and the world of reason, which together form a dialectic world. Living in an entirely natural environment, he wishes for the achievements of civilization, while living in the city he misses the solitude. The reflection on the place of the individual in the world and among other people and also the question of the private and the public sphere have been appearing from the beginning of philosophy.

Protagoras of Abdera (pre-Socratic Greek philosopher, c.490 – 420 BC), for example, states that 'Man is the measure of all things.' However, this is an individual belonging to a particular community. Next, Socrates (Greek philosopher, c.469 – 399 BC) appreciates the city as a place appropriate for an individual and assumes that in the city we do not lose our privacy. For Plato (Greek philosopher, 427 – 347 BC), the state is a necessity. It is created because of the division of labour and the exchange of goods and services taking place there. In this state different tasks are for the ruler, others for soldiers, and others for farmers and craftsmen. The individual in the group is to be brought up to serve the common good the best he can. City life is not a threat to individual development, but a spur to improvement. In this concept there is no room for privacy or for personal space that belongs only to one individual and to which nobody has access to: the individual lives in order to serve the larger collective. Another concept which highlights the advantages of the community life is presented by Aristotle (Greek philosopher, c. 384 – 322 BC). The individual is a political being, who must,

1 Bennet 2008, 4.
2 Schoeman 1992.

therefore, live in political structures. Hence it is evident that the state is a creation of nature and that the man is by nature a political animal. And he, who by nature and not by mere accident is without a state, is either a bad man or above individuality.[3] The state for Aristotle is 'the union of families and villages in a perfect and self-sufficing life'.[4] The individual evolves through biological and family life, in the community life and in the *polis*, which is the end of the development of the individual identity.

In the Renaissance, numerous utopias came into being. Among the utopians there were also eulogists of the city, who believed that the urban space is a place where individuals' privacy is not compromised in any way. In 'New Atlantis', Francis Bacon (British philosopher, c. 1561 – 1626) speaks of a good society which is divided into scientists, engineers and politicians. The scientists create theories, the engineers make machines and the politicians implement them in life. The machines are to change the world for the better in every respect. Bacon's concept is similar to Ritter's (German philosopher, c. 1903 – 1974) idea that if there is plenty of machinery, people will devote more time to thinking. Here emerges the ongoing question. Will not people stop being interested to thinking, history, and culture because they will be absorbed only by machines? Will not the world along with the technological progress take the individual's personal sphere away? Ritter responds to this dilemma clearly when he states that no such situations will arise. Also Niccolò Machiavelli (Italian philosopher, c. 1469 – 1527) sees the individual as a political being. The policy resulting from the state structures is to ensure internal and external security as well as general wealth.

All of the above-mentioned thinkers perceived the state as a necessity of the civilization which is understood in a positive sense. The civilization is not a threat to the individual, quite the opposite, it is the goal of all his activities and their best result.

In an article entitled 'Big City', Joachim Ritter finds that the individual is the city being. Like Socrates, Ritter believes that only the urban life allows deeper reflection upon individual life. In no case can philosophy escape from the reality. Its practice in the solitude of the forest threatens to distort the 'illusory and fictitious nature of the shelter [which] shows no connection between the rescue factor and individual social reality'.[5] Ritter firmly supports the position of Hegel's political realism. He also notes that our world has become scientific with the appearance of a greater number of experts. We have been deprived of

3 Aristotle 1953, 3.

4 Aristotle 1953, 45.

5 Ritter 1994, 159-60.

the decisions on individual issues, but in return we are civilized. Our sense of privacy may change and we may feel that our private space is shrinking, but in return we live in highly developed and structurally complex society. Here the contacts between people are deprived of spontaneity, as forms of interpersonal relationships are characterized by distance, which allows for a rational assessment of the situation and other people, but it deprives us of purely emotional relationships. In individual situations, we feel strong emotions, but we do not show them, because a person living in an institutionalized world must act in a formal way imposed in advance. Ritter emphasizes the fact that becoming civilized is manifested in science: in this respect the engineering sciences lead the way. In these terms, it may seem that in Ritter's civilized world there is no place for individualities, whose position and function would be seriously threatened. According to Ritter this is a false dilemma since only in a civilized environment can any individual values be fully developed and implemented. The anxiety is rather the result of the difficulties in adapting to the changing conditions.

The idea stating that the individual is a solitary being, whose privacy is at stake in contacts with others, and that the civilization is a manifestation of evil, has been rooted in antiquity. The individualistic concept was supported by Epicureans,[6] who believed that that there is no social bond between people, because everyone thinks only about himself.[7] The society was perceived by the Epicureans as a collection of individuals, and the ideal was a solitary life or a life within a group of friends rather than in political communities: 'The time when most of you should most of all withdraw into yourself is when you are forced to be in a crowd'.[8] Other people threaten us and destroy our identity. Life in the community is hypocrisy, a conduct contrary to the individual nature: 'Be not deceived; be not seduced and mistaken. There is no natural tie between reasonable beings. Believe me. Those who say otherwise mislead and impose upon you'.[9]

Jean-Jacques Rousseau (Swiss philosopher, c. 1712 – 1778) too discussed the solitude and the state of nature associated with happiness. The individual being in the state of nature and living in isolation is happy because he has limited desires, and this state also protects him from conflict with others. The 'noble savage' in the state of nature is a simple being, easily meeting his desires, thus happy. Rousseau gives a recipe for maintaining a considerable degree of authenticity, namely, political institutions should be established in accordance with the

6 Epicureanism is a system of philosophy based upon the teachings of Epicurus, Greek philosopher, c. 341– 270 BC.

7 Reale 1999, 269.

8 Reale 1999, 269.

9 Reale 1995, 269.

will of society as a whole: 'Each of us puts his person and all his power in common under the supreme direction of the general will, and, in our corporate capacity, we receive each member as an indivisible part of the whole'.[10] Ritter believes that Rousseau's view on the civilization is an attempt to escape from reality and not an objective overview. Similarly, Friedrich Nietzsche (German philosopher, c. 1844 – 1900), who is an advocate of nature, states that the civilization destroys the person, here intended as a strong noble individual, fully expressing his own life, called 'the Eagle'.[11] 'The Lambs', by contrast, create democratic systems and use the concepts of justice and equality only for their own purposes. They understand equality in a specific way – not as to equalize, but as to level down so that no one can stand out from the 'herd'. In accordance with the principles of justice, you should take away from someone who has more. Therefore, the effect of democracy is a poor individual. Nietzsche speaks on the behalf of the higher individual: 'Oh, higher people abandon the markets'.[12] In opposition to the Socratic understanding of interpersonal relationships, Nietzsche does not care about the welfare of every individual being, but: 'Higher individual is on my mind, he is my first and only thing, and not a individual, not neighbours, not the poorest, not the most suffering, not the best'.[13] Zarathustra considers the big city as a garbage dump of what is rotten, suspicious and lustful: 'A big city is an abomination to me and I already see a pillar of fire, where it will burn'.[14] For both Nietzsche and Ritter, it is important that philosophy is located in reality and does not detach itself from it. However, for Ritter the truth is here and now, among civilized people, while for Nietzsche it is 'in the mountains.' Salvation for the individual living in the civilization 'swamp' is to be born again and to overcome himself. As Nietzsche's Zarathustra, so did Martin Heidegger (German philosopher, c. 1889 – 1976) believe that the place where a person can maintain his personal space and stay himself is not among others but in direct contact with nature.

While criticizing the civilization, Heidegger analyzed the public sphere as a peculiar ontology of everyday life. The philosopher believed that people living in urban structures do not reach the truth. The twaddle is a kind of smoke veil between the individual and the reality, without any grounding in the actual state of things. It only touches the surface of things and it stimulates curiosity for what seems interesting. But there is an ambiguity: you cannot distinguish be-

10 Rousseau 1944, 21.
11 Nietzsche 2003.
12 Nietzsche 1990, 355.
13 Nietzsche 1990, 356.
14 Nietzsche 1990, 357.

tween the authenticity and no authenticity, twaddle and real interest. The antidote to this situation is to stay in seclusion and to listen to the things themselves.

Heidegger's description corresponds, after all, to our present reality. The mechanisms of the conduct and understanding of the world have not changed for over two hundred years. Does the life in society threaten the individual? Is the modern polis to exterminate the individual? Do the aims of our civilization make us flee into solitude in order to survive? Maybe we should slow down and ask ourselves whether the civilization is striving for good, for fullness, for individual truth because, as noted by Hermann Lubbe, 'the crisis of our civilization is not a crisis of aims, but the crisis of control and the metaphor to visualize this difference is to compare it to driving a car. The error of someone, who was driving very fast and because of it did not reach his destination, does not rely on the fact that he did not have any reasonable destination, but because he did not adapt sufficiently and timely his behaviour as a driver to a given control capabilities'.[15]

Privacy and the city

Philosophical reflections on the place and role of the individual in the society or, in other words, on the relation between the individual and the community in today's world relate primarily to the city as an area where the negotiation between the private and the public sphere takes place. As we indicated, philosophers have been trying to determine which of these elements is more important. Two main solutions can be summarized as follows. The individual is the centre of the world and all his activities are relevant to his/her personal life (e.g. happiness, business, etc.). The second approach emphasizes the supremacy of the society over the individuals, claiming that the individual is a special being precisely because he can live socially. Moreover, the exclusion from social and political life means the death of an individual, even if it is not a biological death. The distinction between the individual as the primary reference point and the individual in a social context is crucial, because it is this distinction that generates not only this variety of theories, approaches, and attitudes but, more importantly, also the actions and policies carried out in the spaces where the everyday individual practices take place. This distinction also encompasses a clear distinction between the public and the private as two main ways to conduct and negotiate activities in the urban spaces.

15 Lubbe 1987, 24-6.

Historically, the city was based on determining the boundaries. The traditional distinction between the city (centre) and the country (periphery) over the centuries has not only shaped the appearance of both of these spaces, but it has also affected the balance of power, subordination and sovereignty. This distinction, or dichotomy, also had clear implications for what these two types of locations were associated with.[16] On the one hand a popular slogan coined in the Middle Ages stated that 'city air makes you free'; on the other hand, small-towns and rural life were associated with strong social control and submission to the power of the upper class and clergy.[17] A further reflection of this distinction was also a degree of personal sovereignty of the people living in a given area. The ability to escape outside the control of the society prompted many to abandon friends and generally friendly communities in the country for a city life, which was uncertain, yet providing opportunities. No wonder that the boundary between city and country was maintained in a relatively rigid way, precisely because of the need to limit the movement of people into urban areas and thus to control the population better. But even in the cities there was a quite rigidly fixed system of classes and social strata. It seems reasonable to assume that the degree up to which the individuals and groups were empowered to control their privacy (i.e., to decide on the limit between the private and the public) was a reflection of their class situation. For example, only the rich merchants were able to maintain a large degree of separation between their professional and political activity (public life) and the space of everyday family existence (private life). In most cases, houses were used for living as well as for working: as a result, the public and the private zone were mixed.[18] Similarly, the private life of the rulers and the clergy was clearly separated and protected from the audience. The outside image of the representatives of these two institutions (the government and the church) was meant to signify majesty and power and the disclosure of their private spheres could undermine it.

At least since the Middle Ages urban space as well as the functioning of the city has been based largely on the separation between the public and the private[19] with the public sphere considered more important, even constitutive for the city as a whole. Moreover, without a clear determination of the different spheres and functions, the city as such would have been impossible or would have taken a different shape as a settlement unit. Another important aspect mentioned earlier is the constitution of the city as a political space, allowing the ex-

16 Reader 2005, 7.

17 Hannerz 1980, 63-5.

18 Girouard 1985, 71-2.

19 Mumford 1973, 328-29.

change of information and stabilizing the existing political system. However, it should be emphasized that the city in this dimension as a civic space also drew from the separation between the public and the private. The transition from the private to the public sphere took place with the help of specific social institutions, such as gatherings, elections or shows (theatre, executions), as well as thanks to specific areas, such as the centre, the market, *agora* or the amphitheatre. The individual was a private being in the context of his everyday life and a public (social) one in the context of participation in these events. As it was mentioned earlier, the social position of an individual was a clear indicator of whether a person could be the public being, i.e. whether he had the right to fully participate in the society.

It seems that in the context of the city there were quite distinct spatial arrangements, indicating the existence of a fairly distinct boundary between the private and the public. The freedom of the city inhabitant was based on the fact that despite living in a heterogeneous and populated area, he could largely decide how much 'uncovered' his life would be. This kind of decision was significantly limited in the case of those living in rural areas or, more generally, in the provinces. The simple possibility of transition from the private space of the home to the public space of the city allowed for independent decision as for the 'lifestyle'. Moreover, the character of the cities and of urbanism enables to a large extent to independently draw the line between these two modes. Of course, as it was mentioned earlier, this was correlated with the status and the social position of the city-dweller. Yet another context of the city as such was the violence inherent in the same spatial structure. A clear separation between the public and the private was in fact both liberating and constraining. An element of the ideological violence of the city was based on the fact that public spaces had their strong communal character and were subject to the customary or legal regulations. These spaces were also strongly marked by their social use. For example, the market place imposed certain conduct within it, i.e. it limited the range of the possible social actions of individuals. Another type of such monogenic space was the one dedicated to political activity, usually a part of the market place. The use of various public spaces and a clear separation of the public and the private spaces shaped the repressive nature of the various territories. As we will try to demonstrate, it is also a feature of contemporary cities, in which, however, the changes have significantly redefined the categories of the private and the public. The beginning of the changes connected with the privacy in an urban context occurred in the 19th century as a period of rapid urbanization and industrialization. These processes have not only changed the city as a social and spatial phenomenon, but have also transformed the same categories of the private and the public. The modern capitalist system, closely related to the industrial city at the first stage of industrialization, has been set to enable the spatial mobility of the workers. The availability of labour force was one of the essential elements that determined the success of the industrial economy. This resulted, in an overall scale, in the significant expansion of cities, until they became irreplaceable locations in the system of the capitalist society.[20] The city began not only including increasingly larger territories, but also influencing more and more distant areas. In the 20th century, following urban sprawl, the once quite clear boundary between the city and the country became impossible to define. This phenomenon was evaluated in a negative way and it is regarded as one of the causes of the modern cities' crisis.[21] The transformation of the city as a fairly spatially and socially compact location into the 'urbanized area' also caused the end of negotiations between the city, identified with freedom, and villages and smaller towns associated with a strong social control. This is evident in the case of the suburbs, which were created with the development of Western cities, and yet lived as the centre of parochial life because of their spatial limits. The residents of the suburbs are usually metropolitan types, bound with a big city by means of their work and public life, albeit still subject to public scrutiny, which is a typical phenomenon in the smaller settlement units. Moreover, because of the inability to reduce urban sprawl, spatial boundaries were moved from the outside of the city to its interior. In the other words, instead of the city walls that once surrounded the city, different boundaries were established between the spaces inside the city, for example between the districts inhabited by various social classes.[22]

In response to the conditions that have arisen in the neighbourhoods where the workers lived, several possible solutions were suggested. Among the trends that related to the problems of cities in the industrial era were Le Corbusier's[23] modern functional city and concepts of the Garden City.[24] In the context of our argument, however, it is important to emphasise the disruption of the pre-existing divisions in certain spheres of life following the changes that the urban spaces have undergone. An important innovation, which is related to both the Garden City and the linear city of Le Corbusier, was the division of the city into three main zones: housing, work and leisure, corresponding in their assumption

20 Harvey 1993.

21 Nawratek 2005, 15.

22 McLaughin and Muncie 1999, 102.

23 Charles-Édouard Jeanneret (Le Corbusier), 1887-1965, was a pioneer of modern urban design and architecture. He is famous for the projects of functional Linear City and the so-called Modulor, a "perfect" anthropometric scale applied in various architectural plans.

24 Hall 2002, 27-54.

to three main activities of the modern individual. Because of the implementation of the projects based on this division, the traditional division between the public and the private, largely constitutive for the city, became null and void. Out of these three zones, only one corresponded to the traditional sense of privacy, i.e. the sphere of housing. Nevertheless, housing too underwent some transformation: in the concept of the Garden City, the house was meant to promote not so much the private lives of individuals as the life of a small community. By contrast, modernists tended to plan the city as the society of individuals. Both these ideas of urban planning eventually led to the erosion of public space. The Garden City, transformed into satellite city and then into the suburbia, was discredited in terms of the opportunities it offered to social life. The illusion of the community, created by the suburbia (both in its traditional and current form), makes it impossible to separate the public from the private. The distorted model of social control, which is implemented in suburban areas, means that everything seems to be private while there is no room for genuine social and political life of the community as a whole. Therefore, there is no distinction between what belongs to the private and intimate sphere and what characterizes the life with others. On the other hand, in the modernist housing estates, the common areas are usually the immediate surroundings of large buildings, which also make it difficult to negotiate the private and the public spheres. In a block of flats, what is 'public' is right on the doorstep of your contained flat, but it is a public space by name only, because it does not facilitate the activity of the inhabitants. In her critical address to the modernist city plan, Jane Jacobs pointed out that one of the conditions for the street to function in an appropriate manner for their users is that there must be a clear distinction between the private and the public sphere. Without this distinction, urban space belongs to each person staying in it but at the same time it lacks a sufficient degree of social control, which makes it safe and readily used.[25] According to Jacobs, this demarcation between public and private is one of the necessary features of successful streets and neighbourhoods, if they are to handle stranger and 'make a safety asset, in itself, out of the presence of strangers'.[26] Generally speaking, in modern cities it is possible (and necessary) to ensure the separation between the private and the public, but in such a way that these two spaces could be reproduced and renegotiated in the course of social-spatial practice.

The contemporary city is no longer a social space similar to the one which existed during the industrial city era. Most discussions on privacy in the context of the postmodern city highlight two main aspects. Firstly, as one of the areas at

25 Jacobs 1993, 44.

26 Jacobs 1993, 44.

risk from existing hazards in the city (such as crime, terrorism, environmental issues, etc.), and secondly in the context of modern technologies, such as surveillance techniques[27] and Internet[28], which reduce privacy. All these broad social phenomena are reflected in the outer appearance and organization of urban space today. The privacy-related phenomenon, which is very popular in the cities, is the fencing. It is connected with what is commonly called the fortress city[29] as a concept that emphasizes the need to ensure the safety for the local residents. The only way to do it is to construct spatial elements, which demarcate the space from its surroundings. The most frequent projects associated with the fortress city are gated communities, namely guarded settlements designed to be inherently self-sufficient urban space with the access restricted to their residents and their guests.[30] Although the need for privacy is usually not directly connected with the life in the gated community, if we take into account that the privacy is associated with the possibility of physical separation from the urban and social environment, this issue becomes clearer. The gated communities are associated with a nostalgic search for the community life, which ensures inner control and the possibility of separation between the private life (inside the housing estate) and the public one (outside). However, residing in a gated community is based on very individualistic grounds, and the control is usually provided not by the group itself, but by external organizations and devices, such as security companies, cameras, gates, barriers, etc. Moreover, the membership of a gated community is dependent on the material means: buying an apartment or a house in a secured area is available only to better-off people. Because of the commodification of these spaces the border between the private and the public is not negotiated by the social urban practices, but mediated by the market system and different levels of access to goods. At the same time, it seems that the spaces that appear to enhance privacy destroy also the public or the social life of the city as a specific social organization. Even if we consider that the gated community belongs more to the private sphere, it becomes clear that it lacks a specific public space within and outside it, which would encourage community life. Thus, in this case, the lack of a boundary between the public and the private spheres can be clearly seen as well as the possibility of negotiations between the social spheres in the urban space.

Another very important element in shaping the modern city, connected to the commodification and privacy issues, is the increasing importance of the hy-

---

27 Rule 2007.

28 Solove 2004.

29 Cf. e.g. the description of the Fortress Los Angeles in Davis 2006.

30 Low 2003, 12-3.

perreality of the city. Edward Soja introduced the term SimCity to indicate the transfer of important aspects of urbanism into the realm of virtual reality.[31] This context is connected directly with compromising privacy in the information age with its easy access to the Internet and cultural production.[32] In this context the phenomenon of the privacy erosion is more complex, because it is associated with the mingling of the virtual sphere with the real one, the imaginary with the real. If the city is mediated by modern media, it becomes very difficult to define the spheres of a person's private and public life, especially in the urban spaces. This continuous participation in the virtual world also causes the weakening of the category of privacy itself. In other words, the boundary disappears and so does the possibility to choose between disclosing and hiding an individual's activity. In view of the fact that it is combined with the cultural industry, it is also largely commodified. This is the reason why there are very different access levels, depending not only on the competence of the users, but also on their affluence. Anyhow, the inclusion of people in the virtual life of the city makes their privacy and the public influenced by the external system, which does not offer a clear demarcation, and in consequence it neither protects privacy nor encourages a public activity. If everything is immediately public and private, there is a small margin left, within which you can negotiate your public and private life.

Philosophical categories discussed in the first part of the article seem not to fully encompass the definition of the private and public dimension of the individual's life. In order to use again the Aristotelian distinction between the political individual (public) and the biological one (private), the boundaries between these dimensions need to be strengthened. This would result in some benefits for the privacy of the contemporary individuals as well as for the political and social dimension of public life. The clearer demarcation between the public and the private would potentially facilitate the political and citizen sphere and also protect the private lives of the individuals from commercialization and the power of capitalist relations.

Bibliography

Aristotle 1958. *Politics*. Wroclaw: PWN.

Bennet C. J. 2008. *The Privacy Advocates. Resisting the Spread of Surveillance*. Cambridge MA and London: MIT Press.

Davis M. 2006. *City of Quartz. Excavating the Future in Los Angeles*. London: Verso.

31 Soja 2000.

32 Henderson 2006.

Girouard M. 1985. *Cities and People. A Social and Architectural History*. New Haven & London: Yale University Press.
Hall P. 2002. *Urban and Regional Planning*. London and New York: Routledge.
Hannerz U. 1980. *Exploring the City. Inquiries Toward an Urban Anthropology*. New York: Columbia University Press.
Harvey, D. 1993. *Social Justice and the City*. Oxford: Blackwell.
Hegel G.W.F. 1969. *Elements of the Philosophy of Rights*. Warsaw: PWN.
Henderson H. 2006. *Privacy in the Information Age*. New York: Facts On File.
Jacobs J. 1993. *The Death and Life of Great American Cities*. New York: The Modern Library.
Low S. 2003. *Behind the Gates. Life, Security and the Pursuit of Happiness in Fortress America*. New York and London: Routledge.
Lubbe H. 1987. *The Help is Civilization*, trans. E. Paczkowska- Lagowska. In: Zdanie 7-8, 12, 24-6.
McLaughin E. and Muncie J. 1999. 'Walled Cities. Surveillance, Regulation and Segregation'. In: S. Piley, C. Brook and G. Money (eds.) *Unruly Cities? Order Disorder*. London and New York: Routledge. 96-137.
Mumford L. 1973. *The City in History*. Harmondsworth, Ringwood: Penguin Books.
Nawratek K. 2005. *Miasto jako idea polityczna. [City as a Political Idea]*. Kraków: Korporacja Ha!art.
Nietzsche F. 1990. *Thus Spoke Zarathustra*. Warsaw: PWN.
Nietzsche F. 2003. *On the Genealogy of Morality*. Cracow: Zielona Sowa.
Plato 1958. *Socratic Dialogues*. Warsaw: PWN.
Reader J. 2005. *Cities*. London, Sydney, Glenfield, Parktown: Vintage Books.
Reale G. 1999. *The History of Ancient Philosophy*. Lublin: Redakcja Wydawnictw KUL.
Ritter J. 1994. 'The Big City'. *Philosophical Quarterly*, XXII, 4, 1230-4050.
Rousseau, J. J. 1944. *On the Social Contract*. Łódź: Marian Ginter.
Rule J. B. 2007. *Privacy in Peril*. Oxford: University Press.
Schoeman F. D. 1992. *Privacy and Social Freedom*. Cambridge: Cambridge University Press.
Soja E. W. 2000. *Postmetropolis. Critical Studies of Cities and Regions*. Malden, Oxford, Victoria: Routledge.
Solove D. J. 2004. *The Digital Person. Technology and Privacy in the Information Age*. New York & London: New York University Press.

Privacy and depth configurations. Proximity, permeability and territorial boundaries in urban projects

Kris W. B. Scheerlinck

Abstract

In this paper, depth is considered the main parameter to measure the quality of urban space: it refers to the gradual sequence between adjacent, overlapped or integrated private or public territories in urban projects. This paper pronounces a theoretical and conceptual discourse about the organisation and depth of collective spaces, tested by rereading historical and contemporary urban projects. Theories and models of proximity, permeability and territorial boundaries are linked with the idea of depth configurations in architecture (considering different depth sequences as simultaneous and multiple experiences and inherent organisations of space), together with their spatial, social, cultural and environmental conditions. Privacy (understood as the desire or need to avoid sharing space) is one of the main issues in this discourse, as it depends on the level of collectiveness within a depth configuration, more than the level of explicitness of defined territorial boundaries. This paper wants to prove that depth configurations (and levels of privacy) are not exclusively based on the traditional private/public property distinction but depend on the amount, the nature and the structural qualities of collective space, together with several spacing mechanisms. The urban project's quality depends on the multiplicity of the depth configuration: multiple reading of the space's permeability enriches the urban experience on an individual and a collective level. In other words, the concept of depth configurations does not define a simple morphological discourse about linear quantitative sequences of crossing boundaries: the designing or reading of depth is placed within a more complex configuration of proximity, permeability, integration values and delimiting boundaries on a physical, visual and territorial level.

Privacy is related to depth: privacy, understood as the desire or need to avoid sharing space, can be considered an essential part of depth sequences in architecture. The illustrated urban sequences operating at different scales (Fig.1) demand a rather plural and non-judgemental discourse of coding and decoding depth sequences in architecture. As the examples show, some of them representing sequences in poor and dense residential neighbourhoods in Barcelona (second line), others referring to the popular 'Melrose Place' typology in California, where rich kids share expensive and exclusive properties (fourth line), different models of proximity and permeability produce different types of depth sequence in urban space. Depending on the case, these sequences can be long or short, intense or boring, obtain an irregular or a flat profile, allow slow or fast movements, have a linear or a rather multiple structure and can gradually or irregularly increase or decrease levels of privacy. We could state that it is the very need (or desire) for privacy drives territorial mechanisms in space: multiple agents operate at different scales to provide a variety of models of depth in contemporary landscapes, describing sequences zigzagging between public and private spaces. However, it is important to consider the distinctions between public and private spaces as complex devices, used in many ways, as they are more than single physical barriers in urban space.

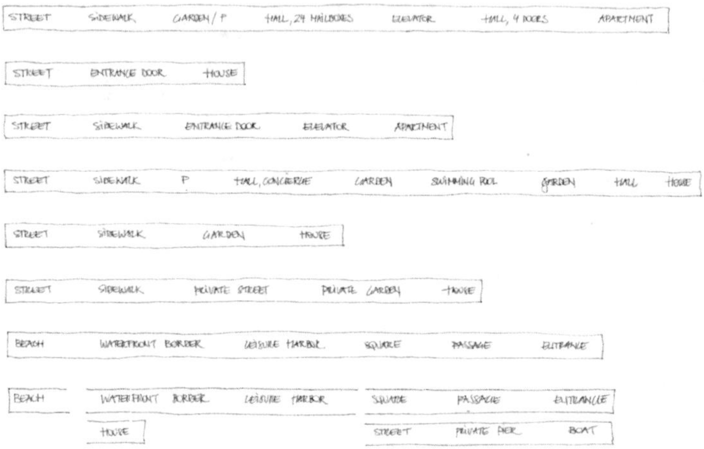

Fig. 1: *Examples of different housing typologies or urban projects, illustrating depth sequences starting from a more public level (the street) to the most private one (the entrance to a residence) (by Kris Scheerlinck)*

This paper pronounces a theoretical and conceptual discourse about the organisation and depth of collective spaces, tested by rereading historical and contemporary urban projects. Theories and models of proximity, permeability and territorial boundaries are linked with the idea of depth configurations in architecture (considering different depth sequences as simultaneous and multiple experiences and inherent organisations of space), together with their spatial, social, cultural and environmental conditions.

Privacy is one of the main issues in this discourse, as it depends on the level of collectiveness within a depth configuration, more than the level of explicitness of defined territorial boundaries.

Depth

The relation between private and public spaces is defined by sequences with different lengths, different intensities and various ways of reading them. According to Habraken, the built environment is defined by a territorial organization and is founded on the principle of inclusion within other territories. The author presents a diagram to relate this very principle of inclusion to transitions between private and public spaces (Fig. 2). Imagining different ways to access those theoretical territories, Habraken defines the concept of 'territorial depth':

> 'Territorial depth is measured by the number of boundary crossings (…) needed to move from the outer space to the innermost territory'[1]

As a result, territorial depth increases when collective spaces (like shared vestibules, common gardens, etc.) are introduced within the multiple sequences. However, territorial depth is not a static parameter: within a certain time framework, after the intervention of various urban agents, depth can increase or decrease in time, according to the specific characteristics and dynamics of the built environment.

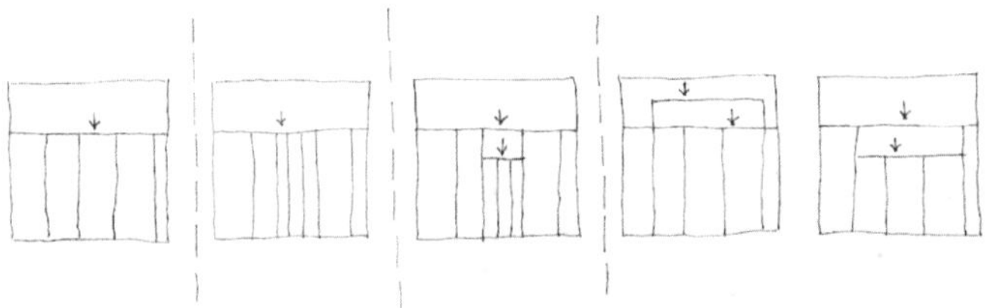

Fig. 2: *Increase in territorial depth, considering the strip indicated in the above part of the diagrams as public space and the below part as private space (diagram made after Habraken 1998, 215, fig. 12.8)*

Habraken relates the possible increase in territorial depth to changing density. The diagrams in Fig. 2 describe different scenarios of increasing depth: the first one from the left represents a system of simple included territories. Starting from this basic territorial division, different scenarios are explained. Increasing density sometimes leads to nothing more than an intensification of available private space (second scheme to the left): territorial depth is not increased, unlike the process of densification. However, in some cases,

1 Habraken 1998, 137.

densification does generate an increase in territorial depth (third scheme, in the middle). Besides intensification of use, meaning subdivision of territory, a zone of shared or collective space was created before entering the new individual territories. Here, territorial depth increases as you cross more boundaries when you 'move from outer space to innermost territories'.[2] In the following scheme (second to the right) we see how included territories occupy public space to make it their own, while the last diagram explains how included territories sometimes sacrifice some of their own space to create shared space. These two scenarios do not contemplate densification of the urban system to increase depth. In other words, increasing depth is directly related to the creation of collective or shared spaces at different levels within the territorial hierarchy. Shared spaces can be common courtyards or vestibules, gardens, storage or parking spaces, common playgrounds, corridors or passages. Some parts of the home can be seen as collective spaces as well, as the inhabitants accept to collectively appropriate those spaces.

Territorial depth is strongly related to the property structure within the hierarchy, even not exclusively dependent on it.

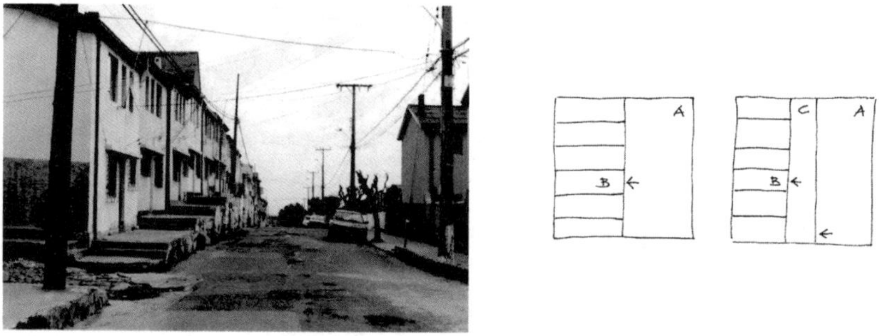

Fig. 3: *An example of increased territorial depth in Valparaiso, Chile. The territories 'A' refer to the most collectively used space, 'B' to the most individually used space, 'C' as the additionally collective space. (diagram made after photographs in situ, Valparaiso, Chile, 2002, photo by Kris Scheerlinck, 2002)*

The idea of increased territorial depth is visible and readable in many urban projects, at a small scale as well as at a bigger scale, within different cultural contexts. In some cases, projects are designed or laid out in an intentioned way to increase or decrease depth, while in some other cases depth is a consequence of external factors like pre-existing site conditions. A case where topography or

2 Habraken 1998, 137.

the absence of rational planning regulations caused an increase of territorial depth is in some neighbourhoods in the city of Valparaiso, Chile, as shown in Fig. 3. The attached houses in this particular street were built before mobility needs obliged to cut through the neighbourhoods and trace wider streets. Obviously, the position of each house is in a specific relation to topography and constitutes a specific territorial organisation of space. To have access to one of the houses situated in the middle, one has to walk up a flight of stairs and pass by the neighbour's windows and front doors to enter the house. We could say that the proportion of shared space within this sequence is getting higher by this configuration. The chance you meet a neighbour or a visitor on a smaller distance is relatively higher than when the houses would have been built on a flat surface, creating in that case a more direct relationship between private and public zones. This particular model of accessibility can be found in many streets in the city of Valparaiso: because of its topographical conditions, shared space is a structural element within the urban fabric. It is important to mention that in this case no gates or fences appear to increase depth: they can be considered invisible territorial boundaries. It is obvious that in this case of increased depth, different levels of privacy are defined by this territorial organisation, on an individual as well as on a collective level. Many other cities, like London or Tel Aviv, seem to experiment with different depth scenarios, sometimes in a spontaneous or in a carefully planned way. Indeed, laying out depth sequences can sometimes be part of bottom-up participation processes and in other occasions be used as deliberate top-down approaches, where collective strategies are used for economical benefits primarily (e.g. higher real estate prices can be achieved when there is access to collective gardens).

Depth configurations

Within the discourse on depth and on territorial organisation of space, Habraken distinguishes cases of dual orientation from cases of territorial overlap. Dual orientation refers to the double orientation that a room, a house, a property or a neighbourhood can have in relation to the more collectively spaces like outdoor spaces or communal areas (like a house that can be reached through two different public streets). The case of territorial overlap however is defined by dual orientation, as well as by the condition that the house or property gives access to a space with at least two different levels of collective use (like a street on one side and an alley with restricted access on the other side). The author recognises in the case of territorial overlap an added value for the urban fabric and its inhabitants, as more appropriation options are provided: the projects, in

fact, can be read and used in different ways by its inhabitants, choosing the level of collectiveness they want to be part of. We could conclude that, according to Habraken's hierarchical approach, depth is related to models of space organization in ever-changing aggregated, included or overlapped territories: defining and controlling access provides territorial control. The author adds that territorial mechanisms are not neutral processes but based on creating asymmetrical relationships: territorial control tends to establish vertical relationships that avoid equal or indifferent accessibility between different space users at all scales. Urban space with restricted or conditioned accessibility tends to be more stable than territories with no more than a potential access control. Within this territorial matrix, the desire for privacy and the need for security are protagonists. In other words, depth is the result of physical, visual and territorial spatial configurations.
Bill Hillier[3] presents a rather non-hierarchical understanding of space that allows the adoption of depth as a relative parameter: the author reads the built environment as a non-spatial system of (non)distributed elements. Here, no pre-orchestrated values are attached to the elements belonging to the depth configuration: his theory is not based on rank and order, as opposed to Habraken's (Fig. 4).

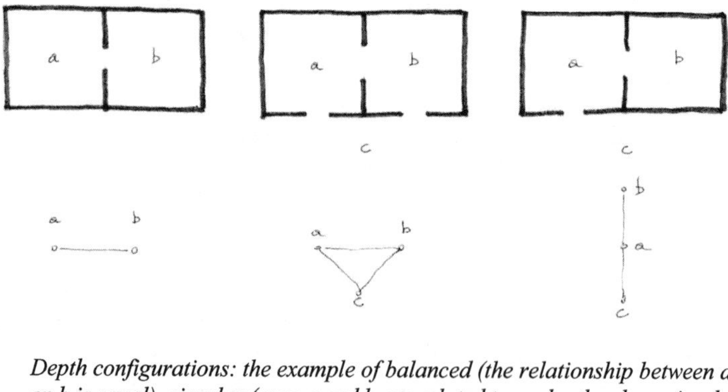

Fig. 4: Depth configurations: the example of balanced (the relationship between area a en b is equal), circular (area a end b are related to each other by a circular movement) and linear depth (you need to pass through area a to go to area b) as a result of configuration (diagram made after Hillier 1996, 34)

Hierarchical structures establish predefined values and inherent specific values to parts of the built environment: access through a main gate of an alley is more important than a secondary entrance at the level of the individual

3 Hillier 1996, 33.

property. Shared monumental staircases in a residential building obtain more structural qualities than the individual alternative. Here, multiple orientation exist, but its constituting elements are not understood as equal: there is a rather vertical organization of space. In a non-hierarchical model, however, the idea of a configuration as a set of spatial and social relationships between different elements becomes more important than hierarchy and its derived vertical strategies to control space. Flexible reading of the environment and its territorial meaning might indeed correspond to a rather horizontally oriented process, where inhabitants have equal multiple options of how to use space. Nevertheless, hierarchical as well as non-hierarchical reading of space and depth both suggest the existence of configurational systems, with several determining urban parameters and simultaneously operating agents. Both theories coincide in the importance of depth and the permeability within spatial configurations.

Related to the idea of space as a configuration of access, a coherent framework should be defined: access defines permeability in private and public properties. We should focus however on the way we use space in order to read and understand the qualities of depth configurations and disentangle the mechanisms to provide privacy. In other words, can we provide an updated definition of collective space?

Collective space

Often, collective space is understood as a blurry and vague space, sandwiched between public and private properties. Many urban projects deal with collective space as if it were a strict synonym for in-between space, for transition or overlap, for interstitial space, always containing a soft and gradual spatial effect. However, in order to study depth sequences as part of physical, visual and territorial configurations, we need to redefine the concept of collective space in a more precise way: contemporary urban phenomena invite profound rephrasing of the theory about private and public space. Traditional public-private distinctions (simply based on property structures, that is, who owns the space, and not on the level of sharing within that space) might not explain contemporary territorial scenarios, where territorial specialisation and market-driven urban strategies define the way we consume space.

Manuel de Solà-Morales[4] questioned the traditional definition of public space: he wondered if public space should be publicly owned to have a

4 de Solà-Morales 2008, 184.

collective dimension, and questions that it should be freely accessible by everyone. The author argues:

> 'It is a fact that the city is the very place where the private domain can be, and often is, a social domain- just as much as or indeed even more than the public domain.(...) Private buildings as public elements, radiating social meaning and value that extend beyond the actual buildings embody their urban character'[5]

In other words, the very nature of the property, that is who owns the piece of land or the building, becomes less important than the way we use space. The author suggested extending the notion of public space to encompass new spaces such as 'parking lots, shopping malls, vacation centres and cinema complexes.'[6] He called these collective spaces and argued that architects should seek broader responsibility for their design: they should not concede their design to commercial logic and developer standards, but rather seek to transform them into challenging new fields of architectural investigation. de Solà-Morales described this task as the urbanization of the collective territory. The author continues:

> 'the civic, architectural, urban and morphological richness of a contemporary city resides in the collective spaces that are not strictly public or private, but both simultaneously. These are public spaces that are used for private activities, or private spaces that allow for collective use, and they include the whole spectrum in between... '[7]

de Solà-Morales suggests interconnecting private or enclosed spaces, to upgrade and to turn them into parts of collective realm: to include the particular into the sphere of the influence of the public.

This new understanding of the private-public relationship changes the character of depth configurations and proximity: this no longer depends on a simple public/private distinction but is related to the amount, quality and nature of collective spaces, that is, the spaces we collectively use. Depth understood as a successive crossing of territorial boundaries from public realm to private one, or vice versa, gets a different meaning if we apply it to the idea of collective spaces. The simple, clear and linear understanding of an urban sequence of approach shifts to a multiple, more ambiguous reading of depth in urban projects. This framework of collective spaces provides an interesting tool to disentangle the collective structure of urban projects, at different scales. A new urban theory, based on the combination and actualization of the ideas of depth, configuration, collective space and proximity, allows a new reading of urban

---

5 de Solà-Morales 1992, 3.

6 de Solà-Morales 1992, 4.

7 de Solà-Morales 2008, 184.

projects, with focus on the collective strategies within. Independent from the scale, we can read sequences, studying the level of collective use with its relative position in the configuration, together with the way limits are codified and de-codified. Within the matrix of collective space, the position of boundaries becomes as important as the way we define them: a comparative study of the position of boundaries illustrates different outcomes for privacy levels.

Domestic sequences and privacy

Habraken describes walking through ancient palaces as 'progressions of halls of great character, yet devoid of any formal indication responding to specific use'.[8] He mentions that users of ancient palaces passed through space after space in succession, as corridors were unknown or rarely used. In a less rational way than we know now, the users settled into sleeping, eating, meeting others, working etc., without a formal functional distinction. The sequence was defined by spatial qualities of smaller or bigger, higher or lower, darker or lighter, enclosed or open spaces within the sequence. Habraken refers to the specific description of typological spaces like mezzanine, hall, attic, cellar, stoop, porch that all refer to space itself, as opposed to functional references we use currently. Habraken calls this the 'historical absence of functional specificity'.[9] The scholar explains that after the 18th century's rationalisation of the domestic scale, a 'fireplace' became a 'dining room': functional specification took over:

> '(...) architecture supported inhabitation by offering a varied topography of spaces and forms. At times, the very entities to which people linked their activities - fireplace, window, sleeping alcove- were themselves like low-order forms, inhabiting the larger building.'[10]

However, besides spatial qualities, there was another element defining depth in pre-modern domestic sequences, independent from this lack of functional specificity: the restriction of access, which introduced levels of privacy within the home. The author uses this references to claim that territorial boundaries between individuals and groups of people were more complex and fluid, for they were less dependent on walls and doors that became the current operating elements within functional lay-outs. He mentions that levels of privacy were neither attached to functional specificity (for example, a bedroom was not

8 Habraken 1998, 132.
9 Habraken 1998, 134.
10 Habraken 1998, 135.

necessarily a space that had to guarantee privacy for its users). Indeed, within most classic palaces or pre-modern mansions, a clear indication was made between private and public territories, or better said, between individually or collectively used areas: from the four-posted bed to rooms, hidden behind walk-in cupboards or decorative walls indicating different levels of privacy. Habraken refers again to included territories and mentions the importance of the disconnection of levels of privacy from functional references: an intimate space does not necessarily need to be a sleeping room, as it is often planned in recent projects.

Drawings or paintings representing daily scenarios within royal palaces or aristocratic residences before the industrial revolution show the clear indication of private territories within the bigger interior space, seen as a continuous public space with temporal restriction of access, illustrating the use of included territories. In pre-modern homes, it is interesting to see the adjacency of collective and intimate spaces without spatial differentiation, without separating circuits of access by using corridors (except from service corridors). Many territorial sequences then depended on subtle access configuration, the presence of abundant sequential gaps, overlap scenarios, but not necessarily showing long predefined territorial transitions. Besides that, we can notice that the most intimate area was not necessarily located at the very end of the domestic sequence or at the deepest part of the spatial structure: here deep territorial structures were combined with short physical and visual depth configurations. Proximity was time dependent and relative. Proximity, read as a coherent system of absolute distances, was less important than in modern lay-outs, as the spatial set-up there was defined by territorial configuration, which meant allowing or denying access with an extreme flexibility in time.

Coherent mapping: configurations of depth and proximity

A systematic study of various historic and contemporary housing typologies (see Figs. 5, 6, 7) shows an interesting range of depth configurations at a domestic scale. For each selected housing typology, like Alvar Aalto's proposal for Interbau Berlin in 1958, a systematic drawing was made of its containing aggregated, integrated or overlapped territories with a later indication of (higher of lower) levels of collectiveness (originally yellow colour, printed in grey): only the most individually used territories are left blank (white) in the plans and corresponding diagrams. Territorial boundaries are indicated (thicker lines, indicating a change of accessibility or access restriction, e.g. between a corridor and an individual sleeping room), together with the detected overlap scenarios (olive green, here darker colour) and sequential gaps (proximity: spacing mechanisms, waiting areas or buffer zones between different spaces, indicated in light grey colour). Within this series of domestic depth configurations, the more street-related area is indicated (see hatch) and to make it possible to compare different projects, this area is always seen as the relative starting point of measured depth sequences. This particular graphic method allows detecting different outcomes in relation to the amount, location and structure of collective space in the studied domestic depth configurations. The mentioned Alvar Aalto typology for example (Fig. 4) shows a systematic decrease of scale of the successive collective spaces (from the middle reception areas towards the peripherally located bedrooms) within the sequence, combined with overlap scenarios at the end of those sequences. In this particular housing typology, the proportion of collective spaces is much higher than the individually used spaces, and is differentiated in plan by a territorial suggestion of in-between space (and not by a wall or a door as an explicit territorial boundary).

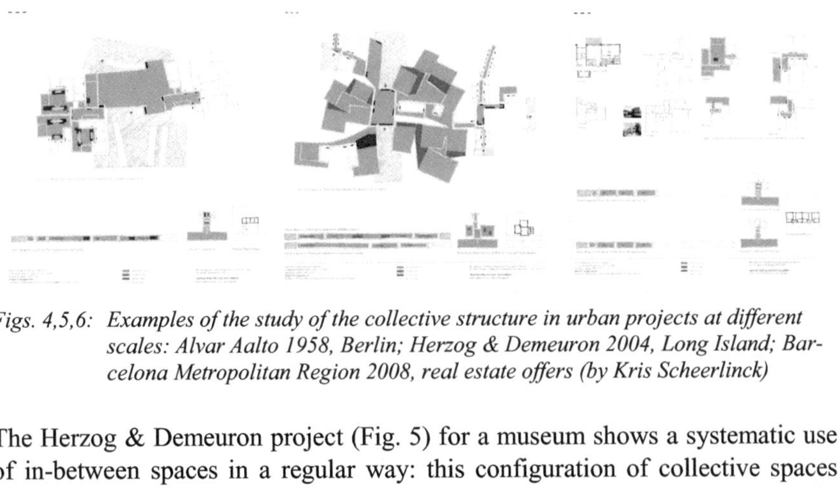

Figs. 4,5,6: Examples of the study of the collective structure in urban projects at different scales: Alvar Aalto 1958, Berlin; Herzog & Demeuron 2004, Long Island; Barcelona Metropolitan Region 2008, real estate offers (by Kris Scheerlinck)

The Herzog & Demeuron project (Fig. 5) for a museum shows a systematic use of in-between spaces in a regular way: this configuration of collective spaces can be seen as a set of sequential gaps, providing a territorial variation within the building. Some part of the project relies on overlap scenarios (the bigger areas, to be used by the public) while other parts (the administration area, based on sequences of smaller spaces) are based on linear and gradual increase of individual use of space with explicit territorial codification (walls and locked doors). In some mapped real estate projects in the Metropolitan area of Barcelona (offered apartments 2008: Fig. 6), the proportion of collective spaces is extremely low, the configuration is based on corridor elements, territorial codification is explicit (no interpretation possible by its users) and the spaces situated at the end of the territorial sequence (bedrooms, separated from the rest of the house) are always considered 'private' areas, which does not invite a dynamic use of the apartment. A similar analysis is done at the bigger scale of the residential cluster, illustrating introverted as well as centripetal organizations of space, or showing projects with more linear distributed collective spaces (see Figs. 8, 9, 10). For each project, an analysis was done to disentangle the territorial organization and the position and value of the collective spaces.

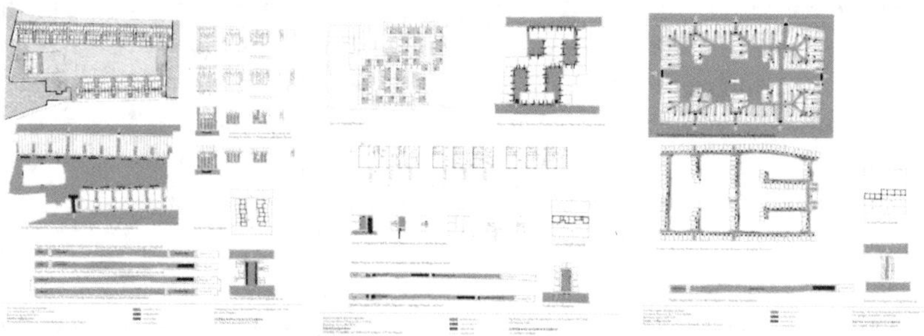

Figs. 8,9,10: Examples of the study of the collective structure in urban projects at different scales: W.J. Neutelings 1990, Gent, introverted use of space; A. Aravena 2003, Iquique, centripetal strategy; M. Brinkman 1920, Rotterdam, ground floor introverted use of space, first level laid out as a linear structure (by Kris Scheerlinck)

The various case studies, from domestic territorial scenarios till the study of urban configurations, show that depth does not exclusively depend on the amount of territorial boundaries crossed, neither on the amount of collective spaces within a sequence. It does depend on the way shared spaces are configured within a project: it is the integration value of the shared space that defines the quality of the depth configuration. Territorial overlap and multiple orientations seem to be important urban design strategies. Increasing the amount of collective spaces does not necessarily increase the value of depth: this depends on the configuration of proximity and permeability of the project at different levels, together with the nature of applied tactics of space codification. Territorial suggestions affect depth differently than explicitly defined sets of boundaries. However, looking at more recent urban projects, a decreasing level of complexity is detected in their depth configurations, with less subtle territorial codification, almost not allowing any user's interpretation. Many urban projects do not present longer or shorter depth configurations but in many occasions obtained a much simpler configuration, compensated by explicitly defined territories. Most recent urban projects show less multiple-choice strategies and are more functionally based. In many projects, the integrated value depends increasingly on corridor elements and pre-planned territorial transitions, avoiding overlap scenarios. The private areas are situated at the end of the pre-planned sequences. In many cases, privacy is only guaranteed by explicitly defined boundaries with no interpretation of the use of space.

As a last series of analyzed urban projects, some streetscapes in Barcelona and New York were used as case studies for studying various collective strategies, some of them as an informal or even accidental mechanism, others as part of a more formalized and intentioned design (Fig. 11).

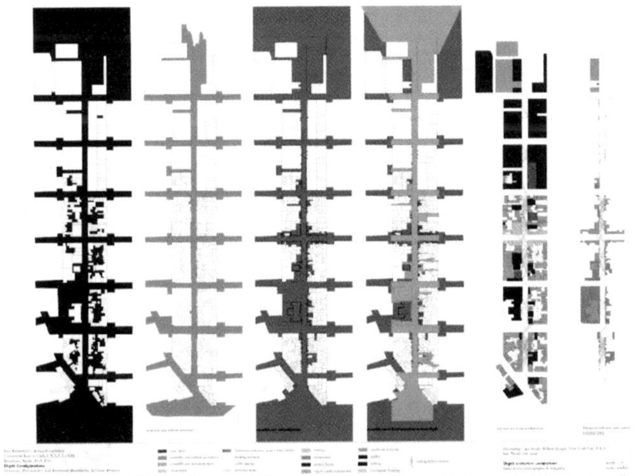

Fig. 11: *Example of comparative scheme of Open Space, Public Property, Collective Space, Visibility Diagram, Functional Diagram with Visual Integration and (Differential) Collective Space in North 5th streetscape, Williamsburgh, New York City, USA (by Kris Scheerlinck)*

Different tactics of delimiting territories introduced the existence of territorial layers within the different streetscapes, where the visual integration of these depth configurations was studied and compared to evaluate social control, privacy levels and the available flexibility of use (Figs. 12, 13, 14).
As opposed to the use of flexible and open ways of codifying and configuring space, some case studies illustrate an extreme obsession for security and privacy, sometimes leading to violent restrictions of access, though not improving any human comfort level.

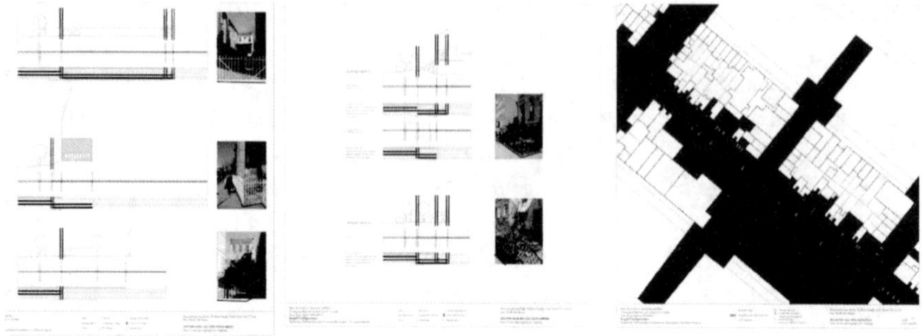

Figs. 12,13,14: *Examples of depth mapping and detail of Collective Space map included ac cess restrictions, indication of time dependent filter tactics (by Kris Scheerlinck)*

The analysis by one of the participants in the MPIA seminar on Collective Spaces at LaSalle (Barcelona), Oscar Chavez, showed a transformation of a residential neighbourhood in Chihuahua, Mexico (Fig. 15), and illustrated how fear for insecurity, together with the desire to climb the social ladder, transforms our built environment, more than traditional planning principles.

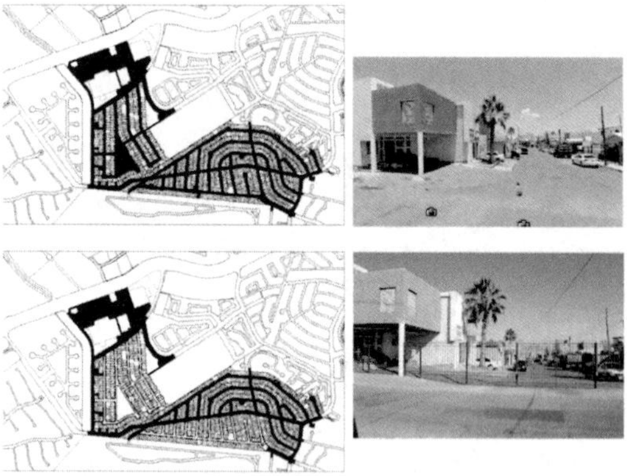

Fig. 15: *The case of Chihuahua, Mexico: before and after the closing of the public streets in the neighbourhood (plan and pictures by Oscar Chavez, MPIA LaSalle Barcelona, 2010)*

The case study showed how the inhabitants of a couple of streets within one neighbourhood decided to close off the streets and (illegally) transform public space into a highly controlled but residual urban space. All owners of a property now pay monthly for a private security guard to exclude unwanted visitors from their neighbourhood's guest list: fences and 'casitas de guardia' (security pavillions) were constructed, all on public property. As a result, we can find some existing property with dual orientation that now is bordered asymmetrically: one side of the property still faces a not (yet) privatized street while another part of that same property does have a 'safe' border. This is a clear example of territorial overlap, where a property is defined by dual orientation and where each entrance belongs to a sphere with a different level of collectiveness (in this case a 'public' area with no access restriction on one side and a 'restricted access' area on the other side). Interestingly enough, unlike the reinforcement on one side of the property, one can still enter from the 'dangerous' part: the fencing off cannot produce more safety. In other words, territorial overlap becomes a case of boundary redundancy. Safety and security seem to have become an image issue, providing social status (independently from some existing threats or problems in the neighbourhood).

Mapping the collective structure of many urban projects at different scales allows a more critical understanding of depth configurations and their socio-cultural conditions: different models of proximity interfere in the lay-out, the reading or the experience of depth.

Conclusion: collective strategies

Depth configurations are not exclusively based on the traditional private/public property distinction but depend on the amount, the nature and the structural qualities of collective space, together with several spacing mechanisms. The urban project's quality rather depends on the multiplicity of the depth configuration: multiple reading of the space's permeability enriches the urban experience on an individual and a collective level. The guarantee for privacy (understood as a desire to not always be part of an all-round collective space) does not depend on how explicit we define territorial boundaries but on the way we configure space, the way and where we define access to neighbourhoods, properties, buildings or rooms. The use of higher walls, building the entrance door at a higher distance from the street, define in a forcing and singular way how people should access or use their rooms, houses or neighbourhoods, does not guarantee a qualitative level of human comfort.

The concept of depth configurations does not define a simple morphological discourse about linear quantitative sequences of crossing boundaries: the designing or reading of depth is placed within a more complex configuration of proximity, permeability, integration values and delimiting boundaries on a physical, visual and territorial level.

Bibliography

Chastain, T. and Chow, R. 1999. *Designing Density. Transformations of Urban Form*. Firenze: Alinea Editrice, FK2.3-FK2.6.

Chow, R. 2002. *Suburban Space, the Fabric of Dwelling*. Berkeley: University of California Press.

De Syllas, J., 1994. *Living in the Community: a Study of the Domestic Life of People with Learning Difficulties Living in Local Authority Hostels*. Athens: NHS Estates.

de Solà-Morales, M. 1992. *Public and Collective Space, The Urbanisation of the Private Domain as a New Challenge*. La Vanguardia, May 12th, 25-6.

de Solà-Morales, M. 1992. *Public and Collective Space, The Urbanization of the Private Domain as a New Challenge*. Oase, 33, 14-18.

de Solà-Morales, M. 2008. *Public and Collective Space, The Urbanisation of the Private Domain as a New Challenge. A Matter of Things*. Rotterdam: Nai Publishers.

Habraken, N.J. 1984. 'Notes on Hierarchy in Form'. Edited version of paper for project on *Form Hierarchies*, Department of Architecture, Massachusetts Institute of Technology.

Habraken, N.J. 1987a. 'Control Hierarchies in Complex Artefacts'. *Proceedings of the 1987 Conference on Planning and Design in Architecture at the International Congress on Planning and Design Theory*, Boston, MIT, American Society of Mechanical Engineers, 84-8.

Habraken, N.J. 1987b. 'The Control of Complexity'. *Places*, 4.2, 5-12.

Habraken, N.J. 1998. *The Structure of the Ordinary*. Cambridge: MIT Press Cambridge.

Habraken, N.J. 2002. 'The Use of Levels'. Keynote Address Unesco Regional Seminar, Seoul, 1988, re-issued *Open House International*, 27.2.

Hanson, J. 1998. *Decoding Homes and Houses*. Cambridge UK: Cambridge University Press.

Hillier, B. 1996. *Space is the Machine*. Cambridge UK: Cambridge University Press.

Hillier, B. and Hanson, J. 1984. *The Social Logic of Space*. Cambridge UK: Cambridge University Press.

Mackay, D. 1980. *Viviendas Plurifamiliares, De la Agregación a la Integración*. Barcelona: Gustavo Gili.

Madanipour, A. 2003. *Public and Private Spaces of the City*. London: Routledge.

Monteiro, C. 1997. 'Activity Analysis in Houses of Recife, Brasil'. *Proceedings of the First Space Syntax Conference* 2, 6-9.

Peatross, F. 1997. 'The Spatial Dimension of Control in Restrictive Settings'. *Proceedings of the First International Space Syntax Conference* 2, 12-15.

Scheerlinck, K. 2010. *Depth Configurations. Proximity, Permeability and Territorial Boundaries in Urban Projects*. Doctoral thesis published at http://www.tesisenxarxa.net/TDX-0203110-102626/

Privacy, photography, and the art defense

Sarah Parsons

Abstract

This article traces and analyzes fears about privacy that are generated by photography. When Eastman Kodak introduced their first handheld camera in 1884, they unwittingly ushered in a new era of public surveillance. In part, it was the new ubiquity of photographic technology that prompted Samuel Warren and Louis Brandeis to draft their now legendary Harvard Law Review article, 'The Right to Privacy' (1890). Anxieties have hardly abated around questions of who takes photographs, for what purposes, and in what contexts they circulate. This article examines tensions between these privacy concerns and the use of photography for social activism or artistic expression.

In early February 2009, Facebook quietly made a change to their terms of service stating that, even after a user had deleted their account, Facebook retained the rights to their content and could continue to circulate, display or otherwise use archived user information. After a blog post on *The Consumerist* website, major news outlets picked up the story and Facebook users started protest groups whose membership quickly numbered in the tens of thousands. Despite the huge commercial potential of the user information, including photographs, held in the Facebook archives, founder Mark Zuckerberg tried to quell the firestorm. He assured his users 'in reality, we wouldn't share your information in a way you wouldn't want'.[1] Voicing the disbelief shared by many users, Sasha Frere-Jones, the pop critic and staff writer for *The New Yorker* deleted his account, writing 'why would anyone trust a company with his or her personal information, especially when that company's explicit legal language claims eternal rights to exploit that information, and there is good reason to expect that they will?'[2]

Frere-Jones's question echoes widespread fears about our ability to define and control our own destinies in an interconnected world that seems to be steadily developing some of the more disturbing aspects of George Orwell's novel, *Nineteen Eighty-Four* (1949). We are frequently subject to visual surveillance through CCTV cameras, screenshots from which surface regularly to serve as evidence of people's movements and associations. Anyone subjecting to 15 minutes of even unsolicited fame may find himself or herself hunted by paparazzi while editors and bloggers source old pictures of them from any person or institution willing to sell. Photographs are an important conduit of

1 Zuckerberg 2009.

2 Stelter 2009.

information and often serve as definitive evidence about people's actions and whereabouts. We have many reasons to be wary of the role photography plays in the digitally mediated, safety obsessed, and profit hungry twenty first century and the impact these photographic activities have on privacy. What interests me here is how those concerns are framed and at which photographic practices they are directed. Frere-Jones directs his suspicions at corporations, but would be unlikely to direct the same suspicions towards artists or journalists, even though those uses of photography may also be profitable and may invade the privacy of others.[3]

Roland Barthes remarked in *Camera Lucida* that 'the age of Photography corresponds precisely to the explosion of the private into the public, or rather into the creation of a new social value, which is the publicity of the private: the private is consumed as such, publicly.'[4] Although it may often seem that photography has participated in the collapse of the distinction between public and private, what is so useful about Barthes's observation is that it retains the two crucial concepts of public and private, but offers a specific understanding of their relationship and of the role played by photography in mediating between them. In Barthes's analysis, private and public are not distinct spaces or aspects of self, but dialectical and shifting concepts. In one sense, what is private is what holds high value in the system of public consumption. In the genre of private pictures sold for public circulation, top dollar goes to nude pictures and illicit activities like drug use. More mundane family or school images of those accused of or victims of heinous crimes also hold great appeal. However, this interest in private moments is not just a matter of lurid curiosity. It also reflects a desire to see beyond our public performance of identity and to make an honest and intimate connection with others. The social value of these private images requires that the resulting photographs come to us through a narrative such as journalism or art that establishes both their authenticity and a justification as to why this private moment can and should be viewed publicly. These justifications or alibis shift over time and context, but examining them carefully can provide a unique perspective on the conception and limits of privacy.

Although we often think of photography as a tool that has stripped us of privacy, it also helped to generate awareness and strengthen the concept. In large part, it was the ease and popularity of Eastman Kodak's first handheld camera in

3 Sasha Frere-Jones is not an activist, but has commented on the futility and oppressive function of censorship in his music column for the New Yorker and on his blog (www.sashafrerejones.com). His position that one should be suspect of corporations, but enable artists to work in an unfettered way is largely axiomatic for those in the culture industry.

4 Barthes 1980, 98.

1884 that prompted Samuel Warren and future United States Supreme Court justice Louis Brandeis to draft their legendary *Harvard Law Review* article entitled 'The Right to Privacy'. Although no such legal concept existed, Warren and Brandeis boldly argued in 1890 that privacy, or 'the right to be let alone,' was a natural extension of the rights established by the laws governing assault, slander, and libel, among others. This was a pressing matter for Warren and Brandeis because the right to be let alone was threatened by 'instantaneous photographs and newspaper enterprise' which invaded 'the sacred precincts of private and domestic life.'[5] From 1839 until the late 1880s, photography was a laborious, carefully orchestrated, and usually commissioned activity that necessarily required the cooperation of the person(s) being photographed. Warren and Brandeis worried that 'since the latest advances in photographic art have rendered it possible to take pictures surreptitiously, the doctrines of contract and of trust are inadequate to support the required protection, and the law of tort must be resorted to.'[6]

Warren and Brandeis pointed to the recent case of the popular singer and actress Marion Manola who was photographed during a performance on Broadway. The role she was playing at the time required her to be wearing tights that exposed her legs. Her theatre manager had asked Manola to pose in tights for advertising purposes. When she refused, he hired a professional photographer to take a photograph from the audience during a performance. The loud sound and bright light of the photographer's primitive flash alerted Manola to the plan. She promptly sued for an injunction against the use of the photograph. In this case, the stage was her professional or public venue. Manola argued, and Warren and Brandeis agree, that to circulate images from this professional space in newspapers, on posters, or for sale in shops was to invade the domain of her private persona. Although Warren and Brandeis do not cover the case in great detail, legal scholar Dorothy Glancy cites contemporary newspaper accounts that suggest Manola was concerned about the effect on her young daughter for whom pictures of her mother displaying her legs and dressed like a man might be upsetting.[7]

While the fears expressed about protecting Manola's femininity seem anachronistic, we still share the same basic fear about reputations compromised by unwanted circulation of one's photographic likeness. Now, we are more likely to fear private images circulating in public spaces, like Facebook, that might devalue our reputation and worth as an employee or public figure rather

5 Warren and Brandeis 1890, 195.
6 Warren and Brandeis, 1890, 211.
7 Glancy 1990, 415.

than as a gendered subject. Just as there was good reason for Manola to be relatively undressed on the stage, there are many legal and reasonable activities that happen in private, such as sexual activity or inebriation, which can have serious social and financial ramifications if represented out of context and in public. Exactly what measures we use to determine our social value may change, but the feeling remains that some normal and legal aspects of our lives should not circulate without our consent.

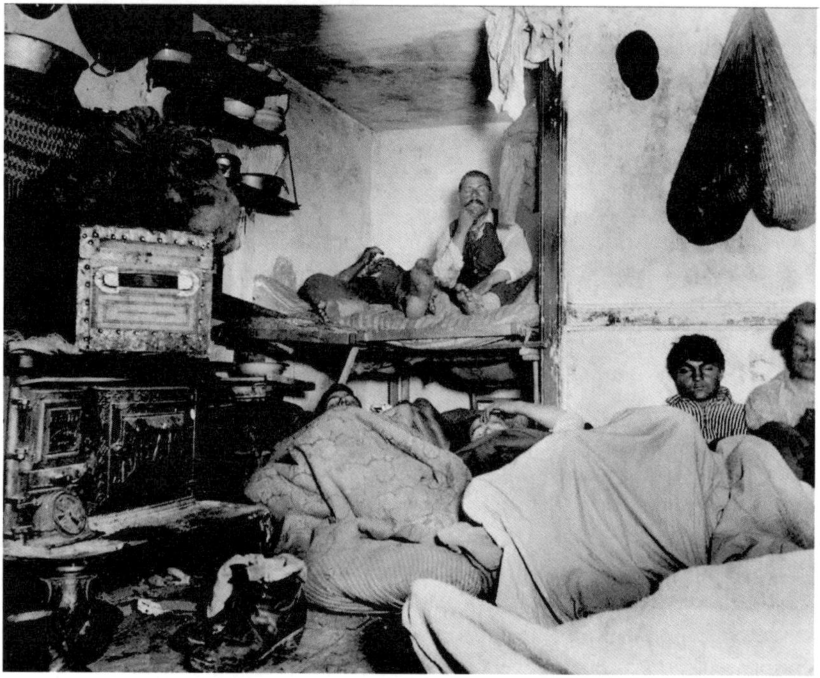

Fig. 1: *Jacob Riis, Five cents a spot, c. 1890 - unauthorized immigration lodgings in a Bayard Steet tenement [New York] www.loc.gov/pictures/resource/cph.3a18572/ (Courtesy of the Library of Congress, Prints & Photographs Division, Miscellaneous Items Collection, LC-USZ62-16348)*

While Marion Manola sang on Broadway, urban reformer Jacob Riis was also hard at work fifty blocks south documenting living and working conditions in the slums of New York. He was so intrigued by the possibility of using the camera as a tool of social change that he purchased his own equipment in 1888. Riis became notorious for bursting into tenement houses in New York City to capture the miserable conditions in which new immigrant workers were living

(Fig. 1). Interestingly, his innovative use of camera flash technology meant that his photographs often revealed more than the inhabitants themselves could see of their squalor. Riis used these images as slide in public lectures and they appeared in magazine articles and in his book, *How the Other Half Lives* (1890). The privacy of these subjects was little discussed. Commentators like Warren and Brandeis were concerned with subjects like Manola who had something to lose when their privacy was violated. Riis's radically disempowered subjects had much more to gain than to lose from his efforts, but, even so, New York law soon protected the right to publish 'newsworthy' photographs even if they might violate the privacy of the subjects. The legal position of social documentary or instrumental photography has remained solid, but its moral and ethical position is more ambivalent.

By the 1930s, government agencies were using photography as a research tool and to curry support for their initiatives. The Farm Security Administration commissioned a team of photographers to document the effect of the economic depression and drought in the southwestern US dustbowl. Images like Dorothea Lange's iconic 'Migrant Mother' (1936) were designed to secure public support for costly relief efforts (Fig. 2). The photographs struck a cord with the public and filled newspapers and magazines for years to come. Decades later, Florence Thompson famously complained of the shame of being universally recognized as the poor and broken mother in Lange picture. Her pain, Thompson said, was compounded by her belief that Lange had benefited financially from the massive success of her image while Thompson did not. In fact, all the FSA photographs were the property of the US government. Lange made no more money from that image than she did off any others for this project, but Thompson's understanding of the public arena as a marketplace in which images circulate as commodities is certainly understandable. Thompson's specific objections came long after Lange's death and gave her no opportunity to respond, but in recollecting the day the photograph was made, Lange wrote that Thomson was cooperative because on some level she understood the photograph could help her and those sharing her plight during the dustbowl and depression.

For Riis and Lange, the social value of the private lent authenticity to their efforts. The success of these efforts required that these 'authentic scenes' be consumed publicly. The photographs need to be discussed and acted upon in order to justify their production and circulation. But, for Thompson, the value of her image and its public consumption take on literal, economic resonance. In her view, her likeness became a commodity that circulated in the public marketplace without benefit to her. Although Lange and Thompson were both referencing ethical issues raised by the same photograph, they focused on different moments in the process. In a sense, they are talking about distinct aspects of photography.

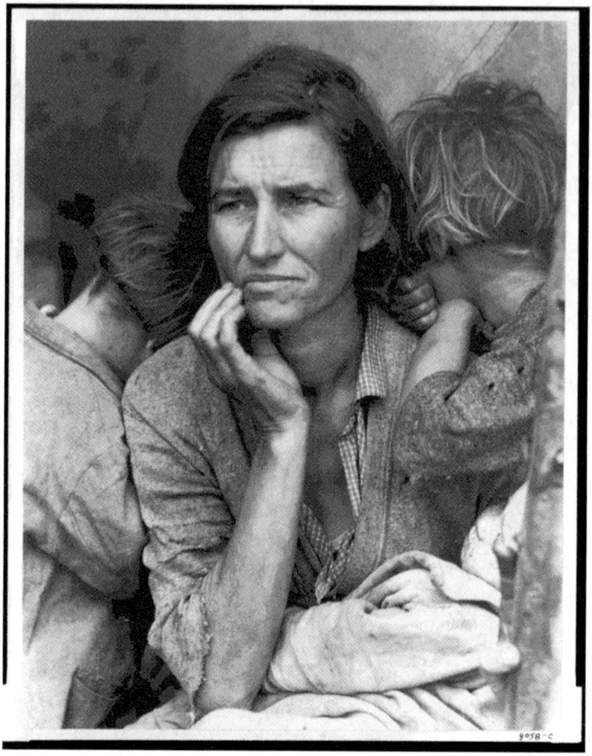

Fig. 2: Dorothea Lange's Migrant Mother, 1936 (Courtesy of the Library of Congress, Prints & Photographs Division, FSA/OWI Collection, LC-USF34- 009058-C)

It is important to consider the distinction between the privacy issues raised in the moment of taking a photograph (which was what Lange describes) and the act of circulating it (which was Thompson's focus). In the age of cell phone cameras and instant communication, this distinction may seem to have collapsed into one moment, but in ethical terms this distinction is an important one to analyze carefully and Nan Goldin's work produced many decades later provides a useful case study in this regard.

Few of Nan Goldin's photographic subjects seem as reluctant as Florence Thompson, but the reception of Goldin's work is shaped by the complex history of social documentary photography. Goldin's subjects seem variously coy, enamored by the attention, indifferent, or too drunk or drugged out to notice. *The Ballad of Sexual Dependency*, Goldin's most famous work, is a collection of very intimate snapshots made among her friends and lovers from the late 1970s through the mid 1980s (Fig. 3). Goldin has described the camera as an extension of herself, a tool she has used since her difficult adolescence as a way of interacting with the world and of trying to hold on to people and moments, which often proved to be all-too-fleeting for her. The photographs are both intimate in subject matter and in style. They feature her circle of friends using drugs, having all types of sex, crying, sleeping, and participating in other normally private activities usually in cramped and grungy settings.

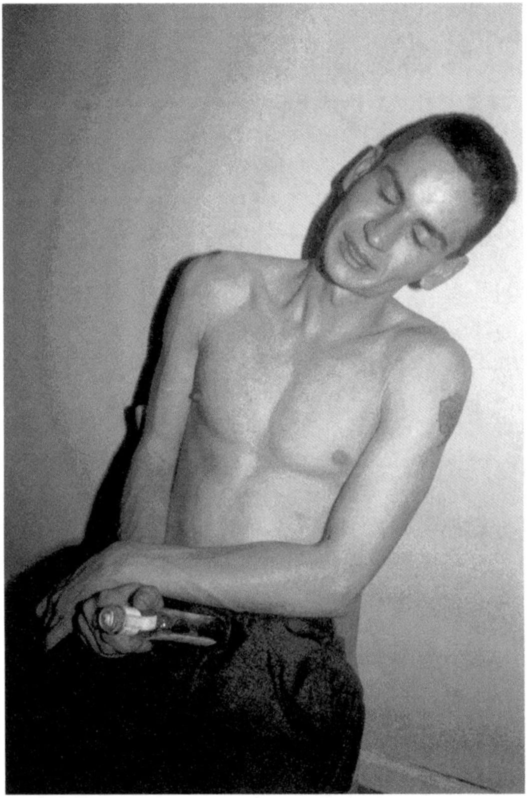

Fig. 3: *Nan Goldin's Mark Dirt, 1981, Cibachrome photograph, 24 x 20 inches (© Nan Goldin, Courtesy Matthew Marks Gallery)*

Critic Arthur Danto perceptively observed 'she found ways of reinventing the snapshot, not in the sense that her pictures look like something taken by a point-and-shoot camera but because there is some internal bond between photographer and subject. Her photographs celebrate that bond.'[8] Even though we do not know the subjects in Goldin's snapshots, her photographs retain their poignancy; they are so raw and so abundant that they enable us to feel we are in that world. At the same time, her subjects do not seem to care if we are looking or not. Their intimacy is often surprising, but it does not feel explicitly performative. It is this intense poignancy that enable Goldin's images to function across wider and wider audiences, albeit to function differently. Her first exhibition venue was Tin Pan Alley, the bar where she worked and where some of the images were taken. She describes her friends as a family and the first screenings of the slide show proceeded like watching family movies or slide shows, with an audience who interject with recollections and for whom the images have wider, shared meanings and narratives. The relationship of private moments to their public consumption is mediated by the shared experiences of the group. Fueled by the success of her nightclub showings, Goldin began to submit the project to small film festivals where it was received by audiences not so different from the range of writers, musicians, and artists she portrays in the photographs. They may not have been actual people viewers knew, but they are types posing in places, roles, and poses that seemed familiar. As Goldin gained notoriety in the art world, the venue for the 800 image, 45 minute slide show shifted from an intimate space akin to the space of production to very public and different spaces of consumption, such as the Whitney Museum in New York and high-end commercial galleries. Over time, framed exhibition prints were added and, in 1986, Aperture published a book version featuring 125 photographs from the series.

Inside and outside the art world, Goldin began to face criticisms for exposing private spaces or moments considered inappropriate for public consumption and circulating photographs of private subjects who may not have been fully able to give their consent. Goldin has long insisted that her work is not voyeuristic because 'voyeurism is closing the windows and spying, so my photography has nothing to do with that.'[9] Instead, Goldin's images are an open love letter — 'and I am not happy unless my friends love them also.'[10] But is loving them privately not different from loving them publically? Is the openness her friends showed in taking the picture, perhaps reveling in their time with a close friend, not distinct from the distance implied in the decision to publish or exhibit them widely and for many decades to come? Some of her subjects are dead and others may have lived lives that are not easily reconciled with

8 Danto 1996.

9 Soulez 2010.

10 Soulez 2010.

documents of their youth of free love and drug use. Goldin withheld images that her friends did not want included, but for many viewers the ethical issues raised by her work and its display foreshadow some of the anxieties around digital social media.

In responding to her critics, Goldin outlines her justification for exhibiting and publishing her work. Interestingly, she does not anchor her justification in artistic freedom (although her supporters have). Instead, she articulates the acceptable conditions under which she feels she can circulate photographs created in private spaces and out of private relationships. In stark contrast to the objectivity Riis and Lange claimed for their documentary photographs, Goldin and her supporters have insisted on the subjective, testimonial function of her work in both private and public terms. In documenting the New York counterculture of the 1970s and, later, the devastating effects of AIDS in the 1980s, she captured the pain and abuse as well as fluid constructions of gender and sexuality. Scholar Jay Prosser argues 'the shift to testimony suggests a number of things: that something legal rests on the production of photographic evidence (testis means 'witness'); and that it has a more psychoanalytic valence. Indeed testimony best evokes the crossing of the private with the public, the way in which history wreaks psychic effects and vice versa.'[11] This claim to testimony is intriguing because it is so generalized and relies on an otherwise dubious claim within the world of contemporary art: that photographs can relay some essential truths about the world. Goldin emerged on the heels of media artists like Cindy Sherman whose work battled against the idea that photographs could offer anything more than believable and often ideological fictions especially about sex and gender. Although Goldin may share the idea that sex and gender are performative, her photographic activity hangs onto a notion of truth and indexicality more akin to the work of Riis and Lange than Sherman. The affective and political power of the *Ballad* is grounded in the understanding that the people, activities and identities pictured are not fictional. As Goldin said 'the only thing I have left is my integrity, you know – and it's not fake.'[12] The *Ballad* functions as testimony and its social value comes, in part at least, from Barthes's notion of value of 'the publicity of the private.'

In Goldin's work, the social value and market value are closely aligned. Goldin's pictures offered a raw and originally aesthetic both in formal terms such as lighting and composition and in subject matter. In the 1980s, she was not just pulling back a curtain into an unseen space, but she was exposing an edgy and even taboo space. For Goldin, the fact that she was picturing and thus

11 Prosser 2002, 341.

12 Walden 1999.

normalizing transvestites and drug addicts was exactly the point. However, the possible political function of these images necessarily shifts as they move from one context to another. Tin Pan Alley slide shows may have provided a context in which Goldin's images could function as testimony or truth-telling, but it is harder for the work to still be read politically as testimony while on sale for thousands of dollars at chic New York gallery Matthew Marks. Once these photographs enter the marketplace, they necessarily enter a different and powerful discourse which is more likely to recast them as lurid commodities of what critic Claire Bishop has called 'trash-glamour' aesthetic (as Goldin's celebrity grew and her style became widely copied, she was accused of glamorizing 'heroin chic').

Goldin herself seems well aware that the line between art and commerce has pivotal importance for the way her work is understood. In 2002, she proudly said 'I never took pictures of people doing heroin to sell clothes … I find that really reprehensible and evil.'[13] (Since then, she has done quite a bit of work in fashion and commercial photography including a luxuriously coloured slide show for the *New York Times* in 2008 featuring rail-thin celebrities dressed in haute couture and posed in lonely, faded baroque rooms.[14]) After her image of two young girls playing naked entitled 'Klara And Edda Belly-Dancing' (1998) was confiscated in England, Goldin felt the need to defend her work: 'I knew pimps and prostitutes, and I knew friends who entered the sex trade to make money to do their art. So I was familiar with the world of pornography, and I always found it distressing and based on contempt. To me, pornography is all about money. That's the difference between pornography and art.'[15] The lines between art and its cousins: porn, entertainment, journalism, advertising, and commerce have moral and legal ramifications particularly in relation to privacy. It is not hard to understand why artists insist on their clarity, but, as a legal case involving Goldin's friend and fellow photographer Philip-Lorca diCorcia's suggests, these distinctions seem increasingly tenuous and largely discursive.

In the US, it is legal to take pictures in public spaces even without the knowledge or agreement of the subject, within certain often-debated limits. Generally, if the act of photographing is not excessively intrusive to personal space (harassment) and the person is not photographed in a private space from the vantage place of public space, then the image is not a violation of privacy. In these cases, the law makes a clear distinction between the act of taking the photograph and of circulating it. Images taken in public are fair game, but, if

13 Garratt 2002.

14 Goldin and DelViscio 2008.

15 Chrisafis 2008, 23.

they are to be used for trade, advertising, or commercial purposes, they are subject to the agreement of the person or persons pictured who might request compensation in exchange for use of their likeness. But, what is the extent of 'commercial' use? Does artistic freedom of expression transfer over into 'commerce' when the image is exhibited and sold in a commercial gallery?

In 1999, diCorcia began a project called 'Heads' in Times Square, New York City. His goal was to take pictures of passersby who did not know they were being photographed in order to capture their authentic private selves as they move about in public. He set up his camera and tripod out of sight and hung strobe lights on scaffolding overhead and exhibited a carefully edited and luxuriously printed collection of the resulting images at the famed Pace/MacGill gallery in Chelsea. The Gallery also published a catalogue in 2001. In 2006, the subject of 'Heads 3' sued diCorcia and the Pace/MacGill gallery arguing breach of privacy. Ermo Nussenzweig is an Orthodox Jew and argued that the reproduction and sale of his image violated his religion's prohibition against graven images. The case hinged largely on a challenge to the notion that art cannot also be commerce. As Nussenzweig argued, 10 copies of his photograph were sold for $20,000-$30,000 each with further sales from the catalogue and thus the image was produced for commercial purposes. The courts rejected his claims, in part because the statute of limitations had expired and the court did not accept Nussenzweig's argument that he did not look at graven images and the mainstream press and thus could not have known about the photograph until it was pointed out to him years later. The judge concluded, 'the possibility of such a photograph is simply the price every person must be prepared to pay for a society in which information and opinion freely flow.' [16] However, the court also spoke clearly to the issue of artistic freedom and to the separation of art and commerce.

Manhattan state Supreme Court Justice Judith J. Gische ruled that New York courts have 'recognized that art can be sold, at least in limited editions, and still retain its artistic character (...) [F]irst [A]mendment protection of art is not limited to only starving artists.' Gische cited mostly circumstantial and material evidence of diCorcia's reputation as a photographic artist in the international artistic community by the fact of his representation and exhibition by a major New York gallery, that his exhibition was reviewed by every newspaper and art magazine of record in the US and beyond, and that his photographs are owned by major museums the world over. For an artist whose work has not yet been recognized, this is a difficult standard. There are many examples of now celebrated artists who were utterly ignored or even shunned in

16 Nussenzweig v DiCorcia 2006.

their day. Van Gogh is a classic example, but there are more recent examples in American photography. A major solo exhibition will open this year at the San Francisco Museum of Modern Art and the Guggenheim Museum featuring the work of American photographer Francesca Woodman. When she killed herself in 1981 she had no gallery representation and no public profile as an artist. She was 22 years old. On the other hand, Gische's definition of an artist would soundly cover Annie Liebovitz. Leibovitz had a major museum exhibition and gallery representation long before she began to exhibit artsy family snapshots along with her slick commercial celebrity portraits. Even soft porn fashion photographer Terry Richardson, who has been roundly accused of sexually harassing and exploiting his models, currently has an exhibition on at a New York gallery and recently had a wildly successful book launch at the New Museum of Contemporary Art in New York.[17] Photography is a marketable skill and almost all photographers do commissioned commercial work as well as work for galleries or other forms of exhibition. Over time, work originally produced for commercial purposes has entered the museum and the art historical canon so distinguishing the two is difficult and often futile.

On the issue of artistic merit, Gische acknowledged that this determination can also be difficult, but that in this case the 'defendants have prima facie shown that the photograph is 'art'. This is not a subjective determination, and cannot be based upon the personal preferences of either party or the court.' Gische nodded to artistic process and intention, but this would be harder to prove without diCorcia's stature in the art world: 'With respect to the HEADS project, diCorcia has described the creative process he used to shoot, edit and finally select the photographs, ultimately used.' She concluded 'Mr. Nussenzweig may have been entitled to if not privacy then ownership and compensation for his likeness, this was rendered moot by the claim of art, of transformation of the subject by the artist.' The actually production of the image is almost automatic so when Gische argues that diCorcia transformed Mr. Nussenzweig through his art she seems to suggest that the art resides in diCorcia's decisions to edit, blow up, and circulate the images as part of a set.

I am not disagreeing with Gische's ruling and I agree that to have sided with Mr. Nussenzweig would have had a chilling effect not just on the future of photography, but on the freedom of communication in general. However, I do think the implications of this case require closer consideration. The legal discussions around diCorcia's images are grounded in a carefully mapped geography of public and private space. Both Mr. diCorcia and Mr. Nussenzweig were in public space when the photograph was made, but the production of the

17 Davis 2010.

image occurred through a process more akin to surveillance than traditional street photography in which the photographer is usually visible if not known to the subject. DiCorcia's practice is connected to the contemporary world of CCTV technology pervasive in many major cities, but it is not critical of this trend as much as it exploits the structure for artistic purposes. If we bristle at the commercial function of CCTV and its ability to capture and archive our movements, it is hard not to feel something for diCorcia's unwitting subjects. In its book catalogue form, the haunting headshot of Mr. Nussenzweig has now entered countless archives – such as museums and libraries across the world. Prints of 48 x 60 inches (1.2 x 1.5 m) hang on walls in as many as 10 offices, private homes and museums around the world, publicly prized for their poignant capture of the private self.

If we are to develop some kind of functional framework for thinking about photography and privacy, we need to acknowledge the complexity of the issue in historical and discursive terms. What we think of as public space is increasingly always/already a public marketplace that swallows up photographs that come to this space through the various discursive channels of advertising, social media, art, or activist efforts. If the end result of a photographic encounter is that recognizable images of people are circulated in public without their knowledge or consent, does it fundamentally matter to the person whose privacy has been violated whether that violation came at the hands of an artist, an activist, or Mark Zuckerberg?

Bibliography

Barthes, R. 1980. *Camera lucida, reflections on photography*. New York: Hill and Wang, 98.

Chrisafis, A. 2008. 'My camera has saved my life'. *The Guardian*, May 22, G2, 23.

Danto, A. 1996. 'Nan Goldin's world (Whitney Museum)'. *The Nation*, 263.18, 32.

Davis, C. 2010. 'Fashion photographer Terry Richardson accused of sexually exploiting models'. *The Guardian*, March 20, 3.

Nussenzweig v Di Corcia, 2006. 'NY Slip Op 50171(U) [11 Misc 3d 1051(A)]'. <http://www.nycourts.gov/reporter/3dseries/2006/2006_50171.htm>

Garratt, S. 2002. 'The dark room'. *The Observer Magazine*, January 6, 10.

Glancy, D., 1990. 'Privacy and the other Miss M'. *Northern Illinois University Law Review*, 10.3, 415.

Goldin, N. and DelViscio, J., 2008. 'Capturing couture'. *New York Times Magazine online*, March16. <http://www.nytimes.com/packages/html/magazine/20080316_NANGOLDIN_FEATURE/index.html?#section1>

Prosser, J. 2002. 'Testimonies in Light, Nan Goldin, devil's playground'. *Women, A Cultural Review*, 13.3, 341.

Soulez, J. 2010. 'Nan Goldin emerges from seclusion with a new Louvre show'. *ARTINFO France*, December 15. <http://www.artinfo.com/news/story/36585/nan-goldin-emerges-from-seclusion-in-a-new-louvre-show/>

Stelter, B. 2009. 'Facebook's users ask who owns information'. *New York Times*, February 16, B3.

Walden, C. 1999. 'Nan Goldin interview, Madonnas, skulls and a lamb with seven legs'. *The Telegraph*, April 6. <http://www.telegraph.co.uk/culture/art/5099705/Nan-Goldin-interview-Madonnas-skulls-and-a-lamb-with-seven-legs.html>

Warren, S.D. and Brandeis, L.D. 1890. 'The right to privacy'. *Harvard Law Review*, 4.5, 193-220.

Zuckerberg, M. 2009. 'On Facebook, people own and control their own information'. *The Facebook Blog*, February 16. <http://www.facebook.com/blog.php?post=54434097130>

Social networking sites and privacy as contextual integrity

Miia Vistilä and Floora Ruokonen

Abstract

Recent advances in information and communication technology have given rise to new questions concerning the nature and scope of privacy. There are many possible theories of privacy by way of which these questions could be addressed. In this paper, we evaluate one of these theories, that is, the theory of privacy as contextual integrity, which has been developed especially by Helen Nissenbaum. We ask how the theory of privacy as contextual integrity works in the context of Internet's social networking sites. We have chosen to evaluate this theory because, as we show, it is more intuitive and explanatory than many of its rival theories of privacy. However, we claim that despite its explanatory power it is not as helpful as its advocates believe it to be in addressing normative questions, such as questions that concern justified claims to privacy in the context of social networking sites. Our argument for this claim is based on the notion of reasonability which Nissenbaum takes to be the condition of justified claims to privacy. According to this notion, a claim is reasonable, if it is based on some recognizable norm pertaining to a recognizable social context. Nissenbaum interprets social media as contexts that serve and extend familiar social contexts, such as the family and workplace. However, when it comes to social networking sites, people often have considerable difficulties in determining to which social contexts various pieces of information belong to. We claim that this is due to the novelty of social networking sites as media. Because of this we should not suppose that claims to privacy on social networking sites are easily derivable from traditional social contexts. Therefore we conclude that it is not reasonable to expect that users of these sites recognize each other interpretations of the context they are operating it. Thus the theory of contextual integrity is not much help in determining exactly what kinds of claims to privacy on social networking sites are justified.

The modern philosophical debate about the concept and scope of privacy dates at least to the end of the 19th century when two gentlemen, Samuel D. Warren and Louis D. Brandeis, called after a right to privacy after newspapers started reporting issues that they considered 'private'.[1] Recent advances of information and communication technology have given the old debate a new twist. Innovations such as social networking sites in Internet distinguish themselves from earlier forms of mass media in that the users of the media also produce most of its content. Coupled with the technical possibilities of the used software, the result is an interesting mix of free and restricted information flow between the users of the sites. Along with this development, new kinds of questions concerning legitimate spreading and using of information have arisen. This has resulted in a

1 Warren and Brandeis 1890; Floridi 2005, 187; Tavani 2008, 135.

need to reevaluate the helpfulness of some of our established ideas of justified privacy claims.

There are plenty of possible approaches to take in a study of the vast terrain of privacy issues going with the advances in communication technology. In this paper we evaluate one of these approaches, that is, the theory of privacy as contextual integrity. We ask how this theory works in establishing the nature of justified privacy claims in the context of Internet's social networking sites. In other words, we ask whether the theory of privacy as contextual integrity can help us to determine what kind of information sharing and gathering is acceptable in and from social networking sites. 'Acceptable' refers here to ethical acceptability, and not, for example, to legality or common opinion. This means that the argument for the acceptability of some form of information sharing or gathering in social networking sites should show that such sharing or gathering is morally right, and not that it is, for example, just permitted by the law or accepted by most people. With social networking sites we refer to sites where people communicate with each other virtually in a manner resembling many forms of more traditional social interaction. The users of the sites can share information with other users of the site, everyone in the Internet or special group of users. Facebook, Twitter, and Google+ among others are examples of these sites. To streamline the discussion we use Facebook as our example in the paper.

The reason for discussing the theory of contextual integrity is that it has in many ways proven to be a promising theory in the study of privacy in the context of new communication technology. The strengths of the theory include, for example, its ability to explain the seeming tension between openness and privacy when it comes to social media contexts. It can also account for the empirical fact that limits of privacy vary in different situations. However, we argue that its strengths as an explanatory theory turn into weaknesses when it is applied to normative questions, such as the question about the ethical acceptability of some form of information sharing. Thus, despite its advocates' claims, it is not a particularly helpful tool for determining the sphere of justified claims to privacy on social networking sites.

The core of theory of privacy as contextual integrity

The theory of privacy as contextual integrity has been operationalised by Helen Nissenbaum, but other philosophers like James H. Moor and Ferdinand Schoeman have indicated similar views on the nature of privacy. Moor attaches privacy 'to a situation or zone and not to the information itself',[2] and according to Schoeman 'we can better understand privacy by characterizing the contexts in which it arises or is invoked as a concern.'[3] In the theory of privacy as contextual integrity, privacy is, as Nissenbaum puts it, the 'right to appropriate flow of personal information'.[4] Here appropriateness is defined as following the information norms that are approved in the context. Violations of privacy can happen, according to the theory of privacy as contextual integrity, either when information is moved within a context or transported across the borders of contexts. According to Nissenbaum, 'in any given situation, a complaint that privacy has been violated is sound in the event that one or the other types of the informational norms has been transgressed'.[5] These norms are either norms pertaining to what it is appropriate to reveal within a given context or norms concerning the transfer of information from one context to another. As an example we can think of a job interview. There are norms that regulate what kind of questions can be asked in the interview, and there are norms that regulate what can be recounted to outsiders about the interviews.

In the above kind of theory of privacy, much depends on the definition of 'context'. How do we recognize contexts and how are they differentiated from each other? According to Nissenbaum 'contexts are structured social settings with characteristics that have evolved over time [...] and are subject to a host of causes and contingencies of purpose, place, culture historical accident, and more'.[6] Nissenbaum also maintains that all contexts are formed around values, ends, purposes or goals, which are partly constitutive of the context: they ground the meaning of the norms of the context and prevent them from becoming merely empty rituals. The justifiability of norms is in turn evaluated in terms of their function in relation to a context's purposes.[7]

The concept of context is problematic in many ways. The theory of privacy as contextual integrity leaves open many questions concerning the limits of contexts and their mutual relations. It is not clear whether contexts can be ordered hierarchically or how conflicts between the norms of different contexts are to be reconciled. Nissenbaum seems to assume that there are hierarchical relations between contexts as she claims that the norms of the context of liberal society are superior to those of other contexts.[8] Yet she does not discuss how, for example,

2 Moor 1997, 30.
3 Schoeman 2008, 11.
4 Nissenbaum 2010, 127,140.
5 Nissenbaum 2004, 138.
6 Nissenbaum 2010, 130.
7 Nissenbaum 2010, 166.
8 Nissenbaum 2010, 182–83.

clashes between different liberal values – say freedom of speech and the harm principle – are to be settled.

The development of theories of privacy

The theory of privacy as contextual integrity is a fairly typical contemporary theory of privacy in that it acknowledges privacy as a complex notion that defies simple essential definitions. This reflects the development of the modern discussion of the notion. Crudely, three phases can be identified in this discussion.

In the first phase, theorists attempted to find either a unified moral grounding for the value of privacy or a single feature by which something – mostly information - could be recognized as private. The moral grounding has been announced variously to be, for example, human dignity and autonomy,[9] human emotionality,[10] or basic human liberties.[11] All these accounts of privacy have proved problematic, since they render the concept either too broad for it to be explanatory or too narrow so that it ceases to reflect some of our strongest intuitions about the scope of the concept of privacy. In other words, the link between the common nominator and the concept of privacy has proven to be too weak to enhance our understanding of its function or value. Theories that seek the private-making-quality, for example, of information have encountered similar problems. A good example is the attempt to define privacy in terms of intimate information: it seems that even if it were easier to define intimate information than private information, not all information that is often considered private can be called intimate. For example, people may see their religious stands as private but not as intimate information. As it proved difficult to find a common nominator for all uses of the concept of privacy, in the next phase of the discussion different categories of privacy were identified. Such categories of privacy as informational privacy, accessional privacy, decisional privacy,[12] psychological privacy,[13] and local privacy[14] were identified. Of these categories informational privacy has received most attention.

This kind of pluralistic definitions of privacy are based on the Wittgensteinian idea of family resemblance, according to which words can mean different things when used in different contexts, and these meanings may form a network

9 Mitrou 2009, 262.
10 Innes 1992, 140.
11 Gutwirth 2002, 42.
12 See for example Anderson 2008, 84-6.
13 For example Tavani 2008, 158.
14 Palm 2008, 202.

of similarities even if there is no one feature that is common to all of them.[15] The word privacy is used differently in different contexts and there might not be a common denominator to all these uses. Thus theorists of the more detailed concepts of privacy defined their notions of specific kinds of privacy differently. Many of the concepts of privacy are incomparable. However, the lack of a single common denominator of privacy makes it difficult to grasp the normative implications of privacy in a way that could, for example, provide guidelines for much needed new legislation concerning privacy.

Perhaps that was the reason why in the next phase of discussion new attempts were made to find a single theory that could include and explain the various meanings of the notion of privacy. However, unlike the first phase of the discussion, now also the multifaceted nature of phenomenon of privacy has been acknowledged. In the current phase, theorists typically aim at managing the plurality of privacy within one theory.

Privacy as contextual integrity is one of the theories of the latest phase of the discussion. Some others are 'the taxonomy of privacy' by Daniel Solove,[16] and 'Restricted Access, Limited Control' (RALC) - theory by Herman Tavani and James Moor.[17] In the taxonomy of privacy theory, Solove classifies the actions concerning privacy - including categories like collecting, processing and disseminating information.[18] Solove analyses the practice, norms and harms in different actions, referring usually to some legal cases in the United States. The theory is practically oriented and directed to help the solving of legal privacy issues. According to the RALC-theory developed by Tavani and Moor, privacy is defined as restricted access which means a person's ability to protect oneself from observation, interruption and information gathering. The second part of the theory's name, 'limited control', refers to how privacy is protected - by securing people's opportunities to choose, to approve of (or not approve of), and to correct information. Tavani uses the concept of 'a situation' to account for the multifaceted nature of privacy. According to Tavani, the nature of privacy as restricted access can be either descriptive or normative depending on the situation. Descriptive privacy refers to 'naturally private situations', such as a solitary walk in the woods. 'Normatively private situations' are guarded by norms of privacy. A medical examination would be an example of a normatively private situation.

Helen Nissenbaum's concept of privacy as contextual integrity unites the strengths of Solove's and Tavani's theories and can therefore enlighten some

15 Solove 2009, 43; Wittgenstein 1953, 66.
16 Solove 2009, 104.
17 Tavani 2007, 11.
18 Solove 2009, 104.

open questions in the current privacy discussion. Like Solove, Nissenbaum interprets the concept of privacy as fundamentally normative. She thus avoids the difficulty of explaining how 'naturally private situations', in which there are no norms governing the scope of the private, differ from simple solitude – that is, what the concept of privacy adds to the description of situations, such as solitary walks in the woods, where there are no privacy norms that could be crossed. This is something Tavani should explain, since he claims that privacy can be defined as a non-normative concept, with normativity entering the picture only with the justification and management of privacy.[19] In addition to this advantage, a normative understanding of the concept of privacy can explain the responses of people to breaches of privacy. The typical responses in such situations are namely reactive attitudes such as blame and indignation. Such responses are also called moral sentiments, that is, sentiments that signal attributions of moral responsibility. Concepts that are evoked in situations describing attributions of moral responsibility are normative concepts *par excellence.* The theory of privacy as contextual integrity shares with the RALC-theory the idea of multifacetedness of the concept of privacy. The norms of a given context determine the content of a privacy claim as well as its justification. A good example of how Nissembaum's theory with its emphasis on the varied contexts of privacy manages to deal with some topical contemporary issues is its take on the public-private dichotomy.

Contrary to many other analyses of privacy, the theory does not build on a strict private-public dichotomy. Nissenbaum notes that privacy is not the polar opposite of publicity, but rather there are privacy norms also within public contexts. Privacy norms might be violated when information is transferred from one public context to another and privacy can be lost also without mass publicity, that is, when information is transferred from one 'private' context to another.[20] An example of violating privacy within private contexts would be a doctor revealing medical information to a patient's relatives without medical reason to do so. In public contexts the practice of mining personal data from 'public' sources can be used as an example. If it is assumed that 'public' means the opposite of 'private' and that what is public can be used without consideration of privacy norms, it is difficult to account for the intuition that privacy is being violated by some data mining. If, however, there are privacy norms pertaining also to public contexts (such as, for example, that it is improper to use public data x in other contexts than the one it was gathered for), the worried responses to data mining can be understood better.

19 Tavani 2007, 11.

20 Nissenbaum 2010, 114-26.

Privacy as contextual integrity and reasonable expectations

Nissenbaum sees privacy in terms of personal rights. According to the scholar, we have the right to privacy, and this means 'a right to live in a world in which our expectations about the flow of personal information are, for the most part, met'.[21] Nissenbaum adds that the expectations that have the right to be met have to be 'reasonable'[22]– naturally the existence alone of an expectation does not entail the right to have it met. In other words, a justified claim to privacy is a claim to have our reasonable expectations about the flow of personal information met. Determining the reasonableness of expectations is not always easy. In the task of discerning reasonable expectations concerning the flow of any given piece of information, the notion of context in which the information flows is utterly important. Nissenbaum claims that it is reasonable to expect information to flow as the norms of the respective context of the information dictate. Reasonable people can recognize and (prima facie) follow these norms. This means that questions about violation of privacy are questions of whether some recognizable norms pertaining to a recognizable context of information flow have been violated.[23] Nissenbaum's theory is essentially a conservative one since the contexts and their norms are those that the majority of persons acting in them recognize. Apart from problems concerning the fundamental ethical justification of privacy norms resting on habit and tradition only, the conservative approach also raises interesting theoretical questions concerning the applicability of the theory to the problems that were the impetus for its creation, that is, problems caused by new information technologies. Nissenbaum's aim is namely not only to explain 'when people will perceive new information technologies and system as threats to privacy' but also to formulate 'an approach to evaluating these systems and prescribing legitimate responses to them'.[24]

Within the conservative theory of privacy as contextual integrity, the latter of Nissembaum's tasks, that is the normative task, seems utterly challenging. The first task of explaining the experience of threatened privacy is less so. As said, one of the advantages of the theory of privacy as contextual integrity is that it can explain people's reactions to perceived violations of privacy. It is a 'normative theory of privacy' in the sense that it defines 'privacy' as a normative concept. The concept is used to point out what is acceptable and what is not.

21 Nissenbaum 2010, 231.

22 Nissenbaum 2010, 233.

23 Nissenbaum 2010, 140-44.

24 Nissenbaum 2010, 2.

Like other normative concepts, it conveys moral sentiments: indignation, moral praise, blame, guilt, etc.[25] Using a phrase like 'violation of privacy' is in itself an expression of a reaction to the perceived action: the reaction that indicates that a norm has been transgressed. Thus, when people perceive new information technologies and systems as threats to privacy, they express the worry that some new technology does not follow existing norms of existing contexts of information flow. Noting this completes the first part of Nissenbaums's task: 'People will perceive new information technologies and systems as threats to privacy',[26] when they feel that a norm underlying their expectation of the flow of information is, or might be, violated. They express this feeling by worries concerning their privacy.

Yet the theory of privacy as contextual integrity purports to be normative also in a stronger sense. As seen, it should also be able to formulate 'an approach to evaluating [information] systems and prescribing legitimate responses to them'.[27] Nissenbaum claims that we have a justified claim to having our reasonable expectations about the flow of personal information met. Reasonable expectations rely on norms of contexts that have existed long enough for people to be able to recognize the norms structuring them. Here we see a problem. Even if we would accept the often contested claim that norms are justifiable when they are part of a generally accepted 'context', there is a clear problem with applying this justification to new contexts. New contexts cannot be structured as old ones, or they would not be new.

Social networking sites, such as Facebook, are a perfect example of the problems the theory of privacy as contextual integrity faces. As media, the networking sites are in many ways new to their users: not only as technical devices, but also as sites of communication. This is evident from how uncertain many people are about what kind of information they should publish in Facebook, which people they should accept as friends, whether they should upload private pictures in their profile, and so forth. These issues are sometimes complicated further by the fact that there are also elaborate ways of controlling the flow of the information one publishes. There are ways of segmenting the people one wishes to be the receivers of this or that information, and there are ways to restrict third parties getting some information. Yet there is no way of controlling all the information one publishes. For example, a close reading of the terms of use reveals that Facebook always has the right to use at least some of the information one publishes, although it is not always clear to what purpose. And like

25 Strawson 2001.
26 Nissenbaum 2010, 2.
27 Nissenbaum 2010, 2.

in the times before our digital age, one cannot always control other people's choices about sharing some information further. 'Private' information shared on social networking sites can be shown to third parties just like private letters.

Social networking sites as contexts

Nissenbaum rejects the idea of social networking sites as a new *sui generis* social context. Contexts are, according to her, formed around values and goals. Therefore no context is likely to be totally new to us, since for us to be able to function in a context its values and goals must be somehow recognizable to us. Against this background Nissenbaum interprets social media as 'serving and extending the transactional range of a diverse variety of [existing] social contexts [...] such as family, workplace, and medical'.[28]

It seems questionable to us that norms of one context can be applied in a totally independent way on any chosen technology. For example, when it comes to such fundamental contexts as family, friends, or workplace, there are some major differences between the information flow on the networking sites and the one in more traditional settings. 'Friends' on social networking sites can include family, colleagues or randomly met people, and some people on the networking site share their stories with everyone alike. It is, however, unlikely that they would tell the same stories to everyone in the same way in face-to-face interaction. The miscellaneous audience of the published information is also likely to affect its content so that it is not quite the same as the information shared in the more secluded and more established social context of family, friends or workplace. This suggests that the context of social networking sites should not be interpreted as serving only existing contexts or some combination of them. Rather, they have at least some functions of their own, and these functions have developed together with the new opportunities offered by the new communication technology.

Besides the fundamental contexts of family, work, etc., there are more specified existing contexts that social networking sites could be compared to depending on the ways they are used. Social networking sites can be used for spreading information - comparable to journalism - or for collecting information. They can also be used as a means of self-reflection - comparable to self-biographies - or for bonding with pears through sharing information - comparable to rumoring. However, all these goals are realized in quite different ways in the new digital world than they are in the media which have existed longer than the Internet. For

28 Nissenbaum 2010, 223-24.

example, when social networking is used for journalistic purposes, there is usually no editor-in-chief responsible for the content. The journalistic virtues of truthfulness and objectivity are not always taken as seriously on social network sites as they are ideally in traditional media. Thus, the meaning of social media journalism can also be seen, instead of from the perspective of the virtue of objectivity, from the perspective of a new opportunity to publish highly subjective world views.

As in the practice of rumoring, much of the information transmitted in social network sites is trivial or compromising chat-like information on what someone has done and with whom. Especially the information concerning others can be seen as rumors, but, unlike old fashioned rumors, rumors on the social networking sites are written. Traditionally many rumors stay in their contexts because they are told only to those who are interested and only with those details that interest the audience.[29] But if the rumors are published in the Internet, social media or magazines, information about both the issue and the person is obtained also by those who do not belong into certain interest groups or know the target person. And depending on the platform, the information can be also easily found also after the rumor is no longer actively spread. Thus, the context of rumors on a social network site is not simply the context of the traditional rumor transferred to another medium.

Sometimes social networking sites are used for the same reasons why self-biographies are written. Some uses of Facebook writing serve the function of showing one's life story as worth of writing as self-biographies do. They can also function as moral inquiries into the writer's life.[30] In both contexts a story about one's life with other people is told. Yet the self-biographical use of social networking sites differs from written self-biographies in that, contrary to self-biographies, social networking sites can be constantly updated. New information can at any point redirect the interpretation of earlier information. Different ways of editing and the possibility of publishing ever new 'chapters' to one's story make the context of social network sites dissimilar to the printed self-biography.

29 Solove 2007, 179-81.

30 Eakin 2004, 4-5.

Privacy as contextual integrity and social networking sites

Explaining claims to privacy

It seems to us that the transformations entrenched contexts go through on the social networking sites provide some reason to see these sites as a new context of information flow. Nissenbaum, however, argues that privacy claims resting on entrenched contexts also work on social networking sites. It seems again that the descriptive part of the argument is more acceptable than the justificatory part. Nissenbaum's insight that norms of entrenched contexts guide people's behavior on social network sites does explain why people often feel that social networking sites are a threat to privacy. Yet this is not enough to actually justify specific claims to privacy on these sites.

Nissenbaum suggests that were we to investigate the background of the indignation or surprise that people experience with information flows on social networking sites, 'we would find that they have understood themselves to be operating in one context and governed by the norms of that context, only to find that others have taken them to be operating in a different one'.[31] This sounds to us indeed a very likely explanation for privacy problems both on the networking sites and in general. If we expect information to flow according to the norms of one context, we react with emotions such as indignation, blame, or even shame, when it turns out that these norms have not been respected. An employee criticizing her company in a Facebook-posting might think she is acting in a private context of friendly joking, whereas her boss might see Facebook as a part of the publicity that forms the public image of the company, and consequently fire the employee. The norms of two contexts collide and both sides are likely to accuse each other of not following the appropriate norms. Another example about controversy of contexts would be the uses of advertising driven services. Users of social networking sites like Facebook use it as a medium to share private information. Yet administrators and advertisers see the site as an opportunity to collect information, for example, for advertising purposes. Facebook has been subject to much criticism from those who think it is not open enough about the information gathering it does. It is known that Facebook collects different kinds of information about its users, but it has never quite clearly stated why all this information is gathered.

31 Nissenbaum 2010, 225.

Justifying claims to privacy

As noted earlier, Nissenbaum not only explains our experiences of violations of privacy but she also claims that these experiences are ethically justified: that is, the users of networking sites are 'rightly surprised and indignant'[32] when their expectations collide with those of others in the same context. Here we come to the questions of what kind of privacy claims are justified in the context of social networking sites. Nissenbaum clearly takes most of the privacy claims that people have made concerning networking sites as justifiable. Her argument is based on the assumption that networking sites are just a new form of technology used in old, entrenched contexts. Thus the norms of these contexts apply also to social networking sites. If there is a question of whether some norm is applicable or not, it should be evaluated in the light of the values of an entrenched context such as friendship, kinship, etc. For example, trustworthiness is important to friendship, and if a person proves untrustworthy because she publishes information that her friends considers private, she violates the values of friendship and is therefore rightly blamed for her action. For Nissenbaum's view to hold, it would first have to be true that social networking sites are nothing but old contexts transferred to new media. We indicated earlier some reasons why this is less than evident, although proving that they in fact are new contexts would require much more conceptual and empirical work and is clearly beyond the scope of this paper. The crucial question concerning the justifiability of privacy claims on social networking sites is, however, not that of the novelty of the context but that of reasonability. An important qualification for the right to have one's expectations concerning the flow of information fulfilled is that the expectations in question are 'reasonable'. One does not have the right to have just any kind expectation fulfilled. So when is an expectation reasonable? As noted earlier, even in Nissenbaum's view an expectation is reasonable only if it is based on some recognizable norm pertaining to a recognizable context of information flow.

We believe that due to the novelty of social networking sites as media, people have considerable difficulties in discerning the contexts to which various pieces of information spread on the sites belong to. Typically these sites allow for both revealing and concealing information in ways that differ from earlier ways of dealing with information. It is clearly not easy for people to locate their own networking site behavior in some specific entrenched social contexts. It seems even more difficult to guess how other people interpret their behavior or how some behavior is meant to be interpreted. Anyone who has witnessed a divorce process of distant acquaintances in Facebook knows the bewilderment: am I really meant to see this, and what am I supposed to do with this information?

32 Nissenbaum 2010, 227.

Due to the difficulty of interpreting other people's expectations in a context with many features that are different from more familiar contexts, we claim that people in such situations often cannot be reasonably expected to recognize the expectations of other people. Therefore to view most of our claims to privacy on social networking sites as justified does not seem fair. How can we ask other people to respect our expectations if there is no established way of knowing what these expectations are? The situation can be compared to the advent of other technical devices: when telephone was first introduced, it was not uncommon that the switchboard operator knew the affairs of the whole village. Nowadays even the police needs license to listen to telephone conversations. A privacy code has been developed while we were becoming more familiar with the device. At the present there exists a clear set of privacy norms pertaining to the use of telephone. There are laws backing up these norms and it is reasonable to expect others to respects them. This is not yet the case with social networking sites which are still in process of evolving into clearly defined contexts of information sharing.

Conclusions

On the basis of the above discussion we conclude that the theory of privacy as contextual integrity is not as useful as Nissenbaum believes when it comes to justifying claims to privacy on social networking sites. This does not mean that the theory is wrong when it describes the nature of privacy. On the contrary, in our opinion it captures very well many crucial aspects of privacy. It offers a plausible description of how the norms pertaining to our accustomed ways of sharing information determine our conceptions of the limits of privacy. On the basis of this, it can account for the variation in understanding these limits. Furthermore, by seeing privacy as a normative concept, it can explain the emotional reactions that typically follow from experiences of violations of privacy. Thus, it can function as a solid descriptive basis on which more prescriptive theories of justified claims to privacy could be built. However, in order to offer normative guidance, the theory of privacy as contextual integrity should be able to take distance from the established norms of existing contexts. After all, guidance is mostly needed in new situations and new contexts. Therefore it might be more fruitful to start the analysis of privacy issues on social networking sites from the premise that they are a new context of information flow. Certainly, after a more thorough investigation it could turn out that these new social networking sites are indeed, as Nissenbaum suggests, only a new media for old contexts. Assuming this from the beginning might however lead to deflating the potential of social networking sites to expand our choice of forms of communication.

Bibliography

Anderson, S.A. 2008. 'Privacy without the Right to Privacy'. *The Monist*, 91, 81-107.

Eakin, P. J. 2004. 'Introduction: Mapping the Ethics of Life Writing'. In P. J. Eakin (ed.) *The Ethics of Life Writing*. Ithaca and London: Cornell University Press, 1-18.

Floridi, L. 2005. 'The Ontological Interpretation of Informational Privacy'. *Ethics and Information Technology*, 7, 185-200.

Gutwirth, S. 2002. *Privacy and the Information Age*. Maryland: Rowman & Littlefield Publishers.

Inness, J. 1992. *Privacy, Intimacy and Isolation*. Oxford: Oxford University Press.

Mitrou, L. 2009. 'Commodification of the Individual in the Internet Era: Informational Self-determination or 'Self-alienation'?'. In M. Bottis (ed.) *Proceedings of the 8th International Conference of Computer Ethics: Philosophical Enquiry*. Athens: Nomiki Bibliothiki, 466-84.

Moor, J.H. 1997. 'Towards a Theory of Privacy in the Information Age'. *Computers and Society*, 27, 27-32.

Nissenbaum, H. 2004. 'Privacy as Contextual Integrity'. *Washington Law Review*, 79, 119-58.

Nissenbaum, H. 2010. *Privacy in Context. Technology, Policy and the Integrity of Social Life*. Stanford, California: Stanford University Press.

Palm, E. 2008. 'Privacy Expectations at Work – What is Reasonable and Why?'. *Ethical Theory, Moral Practice*, 12, 201-15.

Schoeman, F.D. 2008. *Privacy and Social Freedom*. Cambridge: Cambridge University Press.

Solove, D. 2007. *The future of reputation: gossip, rumor, and privacy on the Internet*. New Haven: Yale University Press.

Solove, D. 2009. *Understanding Privacy*. Harvard: Harvard University Press.

Strawson, P. 2001. 'Freedom and Resentment'. In L. Waddell Ekstrom (ed.) *Agency and Responsibility*. Bulder: Westview Press, 183-204. Originally published in *Proceedings of the British Academy*, 48 (1960) 1-25.

Tavani, H.T. 2007. 'Philosophical Theories of Privacy: Implications for an Adequate Online Privacy Policy'. *Metaphilosophy*, 38, 1-22.

Tavani, H.T. 2008. 'Informational Privacy: Concepts, Theories and Controversies'. In *The Handbook of Information and Computer Ethics*. Hoboken, New Jersey: John Wiley & Sons, 131-64.

Warren, S. D. and Brandeis, L. D. 1890. 'The Right to Privacy'. *Harvard Law Review*, 4.5, 193-220.

Wittgenstein, L. 1953. *Philosophical Investigations*. Oxford: Blackwell.

Private life in bits and pieces: Digital and molecular personhood in the information age

Ilpo Helén and Karoliina Snell

Abstract

This chapter focuses on the problem of informational privacy in the context of collection, storage and circulation of digitalized health and genomic information of individual persons in biobanks and biobank networks. Privacy problems associated with biobanks are juxtaposed with other information flows in ICT networks, like social media, and with commercial provision of genetic tests direct to consumers. The key question of the study is the following: In which way are concerns over informational privacy regarding circulation of 'bioinformation' specific to that domain and in which respects are they similar to wider flows of digitalized personal information? The focal theme of the chapter is the relationship of protection of privacy and personal information from outside intrusion to the personal deployment and sharing of 'private affairs' in public and semi-public arenas.

In the beginning of the 21st century, the notions of privacy and the private sphere are profoundly different from what they have been in the modern Western culture since the 19th century. For example, a basic juridical concept of privacy as 'a right to be let alone'1, originated as a response to the 'yellow press' in the late 19th century, seems to have only a limited validity in today's discussions.2 Decentralized ICT networks for global circulation of digital information have essentially contributed to the transformation by which 'privacy problems' have become more complicated and harder to define than before. With the consolidation of the technical basis and practical arrangements for information flows in the network society3 the issue of informational privacy has become the focus of study and debate in the fields of law, moral philosophy, social sciences, and governance.4 In our chapter, we discuss the problem of informational privacy in a specific context.

We focus on collection, storage and circulation of digitalized health and genomic information of individual persons and population and on privacy problems related to the governance of biobanks and biobank networks. We juxtapose

1 Warren and Brandeis 1890.

2 Solove 2004; Knoppers 2010.

3 Castells 1996.

4 Nissenbaum 2010. According to Rössler (2005, 11), questions about personal control over what other people can know about oneself belong to the domain of informational privacy.

privacy problems associated with biobanks with other information flows in ICT networks, like social media, and with commercial provision of gene tests direct to consumers. The term 'biobank' refers to a variety of social and technical arrangements for retrieving, storing, and exchanging tissues samples and associated medical and lifestyle information (e.g. diagnosis and health records, life style information, family histories, or register data). There is a huge variation in size and organisation of biobanks from large national collections covering general population to specialized, small collections connected to a hospital clinic or a research laboratory. Basically, all biobanks are depositories of genetic information which make data available for laboratories and research groups carrying out actual biomedical research.[5] The collection of tissue samples and medical information of individual persons, and storage and circulation of this type of data in a digital form can be seen as a part of global exchange of biological material (e.g. transplant organs, tissue samples, cell lines, and molecular 'tools' used in clinics and research laboratories) with attached medical information. The subject of our study is connections and parallels between this 'tissue economy'[6] and the circulation of other types of digitalized personal information in ICT networks. We ask in which way concerns over informational privacy within tissue economy are specific to that domain and in which respects they are similar to wider flows of digitalized personal information.

Our study is empirical. We have analyzed focus group discussions conducted among Finnish people in 2010 and 2011 and texts from social media and direct-to-consumer genetic test websites. The focus group interviews were done in two sets. The first three groups were themed around biobanks, while the second set of four groups was concentrated on more generally digital information flows, biobanks, and privacy. All together 46 people aged between 20 and 70 years participated in the focus groups.

Privacy and personhood

As a response to the expansion of digital databases of personal information and the circulation of the data in the Internet and other computerized networks, many scholars have pointed out new challenges for the law and juridical practice in defining and protecting informational privacy. Especially in the U.S., many

---

5 Cambon-Thomsen 2004; Hirtzlin et al. 2003.

6 Waldby and Mitchell (2006) coined this concept to refer to exchange and circulation of biological material (e.g. transplant organs, blood products, tissue samples, and cell lines) and medical information in global commercial and scientific networks.

experts in law have argued that current legal concepts of privacy are inadequate and indicated shortcomings of juridical institutions in protecting individual persons against potential or actual harm caused by the storage and circulation of personal information in the digital form.[7] The critical discussion in law defines the privacy problem in terms of intrusion in the private sphere and upon individual person, and focuses on the protection of personal privacy. These aspects are obviously pivotal when privacy in the information society is discussed. However, we consider this juridical concept too narrow for our analysis, because it implicitly defines privacy in a negative manner, as if a property under threat. Rather, we approach privacy from the view point of social analysis, which considers the numbers of functions and meaning that privacy has in the context of social institutions and practices. It also shows how the relation of privacy to the public sphere may acquire different definitions and significance depending on the context of social life in which it is embedded. Consequently, the concept of privacy has also a political dimension, since privacy issues can be used and deployed to mobilize public opinion and to participate in a political contestation. Social analysis also underlines the historical transformations of the notions of privacy: the significance and functions of privacy and the relationship between the private and public spheres have been changed and tend to be refined over time.[8]

The main regulatory, moral and even technical problems of privacy in digitalized information flows are related to two characteristics. First, vast amounts of personal data are compiled in both public and private digital databases and can be easily disseminated. Second, the individual users of ICT networks leave traces of personal activities and preferences in the Internet which may be gathered in databases and deployed by Internet service providers. When informational privacy is seen as a social phenomenon in this context, the problems related to it are not defined merely as protection of privacy from intrusion. What is at stake is rather the issue of control and management of sharing digital information and the feedback (e.g. targeted marketing) in the cyberspace. The problems are related to both institutional and personal *uncontrollability* of dissemination and effects of the information flows.[9]

Emphasis on personal control is congruent with Rössler's general definition of privacy: 'Something counts as private if one can oneself control the access to this "something".'[10] However, as a part of social life privacy is not just control.

7 Nissenbaum 2010; Solove 2004.

8 E.g. McKee 2005.

9 Solove 2004.

10 Rössler 2005, 8.

When people engage in digital information flows they weigh how 'private' the personal information they share is, differentiate between types of personal information, and define degrees of privacy in their lives.[11] This conduct 'in the Web' can be called *privacy management*.[12]

Management of personal information in the digital world points out to another social dimension of privacy. People may also deploy privacy for social or political purposes by sharing information about themselves and their private lives through Internet discussion fora, homepages, blogs and social media. Increasing opportunities for presentation of the self in WWW, to paraphrase Goffman,[13] make digital 'profiling' of the person an everyday activity, something you can even play with like in the world of online role-playing games. Moreover, deployment of privacy in a digital form is related to the emergence of new modes of sociability, as the sharing of personal information through ICT networks has enabled the maintenance of intimate relationships at long distances and facilitated the creation of Internet based virtual communities.[14]

From the perspective of social analysis the concept of privacy is closely attached to the notion of the person. This emphasis is parallel to Rössler's normative concept of privacy, since she considers privacy – i.e. personal control over private sphere, affairs, and information – as the prerequisite of personal autonomy and self-identity.[15] In the context of social sciences, 'the person' signifies three dimensions of human existence: first, it refers to the uniqueness of a human being, his or her biography; second, 'the person' means self-awareness which is usually connected to memory, i.e. to human capability to remember who one is and what one has done; finally, the person refers to a social role or status. The latter aspect is particularly important. For a social scientist 'the person' is essentially social: personhood of an individual emerges and is modified in social life by other human beings who see, consider, and recognize who and what she or he is as a separate person. This notion is closely linked to the emphasis of historical modifiability of personhood: while the modes of social life, habits, and interaction change over time, also the modes of seeing and recognizing the person will be modified accordingly.[16]

---

11 E.g. Boyd 2010.
12 Waters and Ackerman 2011.
13 Goffman 1959.
14 Papacharissi 2010.
15 Rössler 2005.
16 E.g. Carrithers, Collins and Lukes 1987.

Lost and found in the cyberspace

Since we see 'privacy' as conceptually inseparable from 'the person', we claim that the rise of privacy problems in relation to collection and use of personal information in digital dossiers reflects the modification of conditions of being a person in the global network society. Worldwide circulation of vast amounts of personal information in computer networks has created a novel *condition humaine*. The framework in, and the means by which, people are seen and become recognized as persons have been fundamentally changed by flows of digital information, and modes and settings for presentation of the self have multiplied.

When considering the role of digital dossiers today and their impact on being a person, it should be remembered that collection and storage of data about identifiable persons is not a new invention. Courts of law and penal institutions have filed information about their clients and kept them in archives for centuries. A key activity of the modern state is collection of personal information in numerous public registers for census, taxation, popular elections, and for governance of health, social and popular education. Moreover, medical records are not a particularly recent invention neither is the social security number. All in all, modern mode of government and social life have developed into a dossier society all over the Western world during the past two centuries, with Finland and other Nordic countries being exemplary of this development.[17]

So, what is new today? The ICT technology has facilitated three developments. First, everyday transactions have been digitalized to a great extent, and whenever we use our credit cards or consumer bonus cards, buy something via Internet or respond to a website request, we deliver a piece of personal information in the cyberspace. At the same time, the collection of personal information in public and private databases has become more intense, as the storage and handling of the data in the digital form have become easier. As a consequence, an increased amount of personal information is available in the cyberspace, and the number of institutions, both public and private, in possession of a database for personal information has multiplied.[18] Second, the development of the Internet has allowed an exponential growth in circulation of this information across the national borders and between public and private institutions. Finally, combination of information from different digital databases has become easy and rapid and, consequently, activities to 'cross analyze' and to aggregate personal data from various sources have proliferated, in both public and private sector.

17 E.g. Alastalo and Åkerman 2011.

18 Solove 2004.

Two impacts of digitalization of transactions in everyday life on reconfiguration of privacy and personhood are crucial. First, while massive amount of small fragments of personal information is disseminated in the cyberspace, the person is multiplied and dispersed into bits and pieces in the digital world. Second, the flows of digital information have multiplied the settings and configurations in which people can be seen and considered as persons. The crucial questions in this context are the following. Under which circumstances, through which channels, and by which practices of data aggregation and circulation do bits and pieces of 'personal' information become compiled as a 'biography' or personal 'profile' and are assigned to a person? What sort of compilation of data actually makes up a person, and how do such compilations emerge out of the information mass?

At the heart of the matter is the fact that the information of people in databases (digital and other kinds) is not mainly used to identify particular individuals but to analyze populations, and to define groups of people or types of individuals. The purpose of aggregation and analysis of the personal data serve not primarily direct interventions in persons' lives but are used for assessment of health risks, for detection of consumer segments or for making a profile of the offender in crime investigation. This sort of information does not refer to any single individual directly, although it carries an inherent privacy risk for the individuals as well.[19] However, information about belonging to a projected group or to a segment of people can be addressed to particular individuals. For example, when the customer purchases a book or DVD in Amazon, she or he is informed that 'people who buy X also buy Y'. This feedback is based on aggregation of digital purchase data into consumer profiles. A rationale parallel to 'targeted marketing' can be found in preventive health care when, for example, women over 40 are invited to breast cancer screening because they belong to a risk group. This sort of *automated recognition* by virtual group membership, based on fragments of personal information and digital traces, is an important mode in which personhood is processed today.

The settings in which people are recognized as being this or that kind of persons and in which they present themselves have become innumerable in the world of endless circulation and aggregation of digital information. The data flow from digital dossiers and social media to the multiple settings through innumerable routes is out of control by individuals and institutions. Moreover, since a big share of people's everyday transactions takes place in the digital universe, sharing personal data and getting automated feedback attached to personal conduct have become a routine, even unnoticed part of our ordinary life. The *in-*

19 See Craig et al. 2011

formational person as the individual embedded in the flows of digital information is unsettled, even ephemeral, since the personal 'profiles' based on both automated aggregation of database information and on deliberate updating of self-presentation in homepages, blogs or social media are under modification all the time.

All in all, circulation and aggregation of personal information in the ICT networks are potentially uncontrollable, ubiquitous and create unsettled clusters, which have made privacy a complex issue and also modified conditions of being a person – uniqueness of an individual, her or his self-awareness and social roles – in a certain manner. This condition is characterized by *openness* of personhood in two senses. On the one hand, an individual person is open to potential invasion or exploitation through the circulation of information about her or him in the cyberspace. On the other hand, a person is unfinished because information about her or him is being compiled in the digital databases all the time, existing personal information can be aggregated over and over again, and the new 'personal profiles' can be fed back to her or him continuously.

Flows of vital information

The expansion of the digitalized dossiers in society has created a sort of paradox of information control. As the data flow in ICT networks is designed to be – and has actually become – essentially uncontrollable, demands for stricter regulation and management for protection and security of personal data have intensified. Collection, storage, and circulation of biological samples and related medical or other personal data in public biobanks and biobank networks are not untouched by this paradox, although the way personal information is stored and flows in biobank circuits is very different from the way information flows in Internet and databases collected by commercial service providers like Google or Facebook. The gathering and sharing of biobank information as well as access to the data are quite strictly regulated by national authorities and international agreements. Explicit procedures for protecting the anonymity as well as personal and bodily integrity of donors and for guaranteeing the proper use of the data in medical research (informed consent, encrypting and anonymization of data, protocols for providing access to the data, etc.) are required for storage and sharing of the biobank information.[20]

Health information has been regarded personally sensitive and therefore medical records have been traditionally considered confidential, 'private' in the

20 E.g. Kaye and Stranger 2009.

strictest sense of the word.[21] However, health information has been collected and circulated for the purposes of clinical and public health research and for public health governance for centuries. For research and governance purposes, circulation of information in health registers is restricted to researchers, professionals, and public health authorities. This model is applied to the regulation of biobanks, too. However, concern over and protection of personal information compiled in biobanks are more intense than in ordinary medical registers, since genetic information has been considered to be 'exceptional', because it is about 'life itself' and thought to reveal aspects of the person's 'biological destiny'.[22] DNA information in tissue or blood samples is thus regarded personally sensitive and potentially powerful, and due to this view particular attention has been paid on circulation of biological material and related information by the regulators of the biobanks. In our focus groups, however, people seldom regarded tissues samples and DNA information different from, and more personal than, information given, for example, to health surveys or medical registers. Even though people reflected on many possible personal and societal consequences of sharing their DNA, genetic information is usually seen as just another type of health information. This does not mean that DNA would not be understood as private or personal. Rather, all health related data are considered to be personal.[23]

Despite the strict regulation of biobanks, concerns over their governance and the privacy of donors have been raised in professional and public discussions since the early 1990s when the first big biobank projects were launched.[24] Several features of biobanking give rise to these concerns: vast amount of personal information is stored for long periods, possible uses of the data in medical research in the future are unknown, and tissue samples and data circulate across the institutional and national borders.[25] The problems of privacy protection and governance of biobanking have become more complex, as the technological vision of biobanks has changed from national organization of sample and information collection to transnational biobank infrastructures for circulation of biomaterial and information.[26] With these developments biobanking is transforming into flows of vital information which contain an element of uncontrollability, since the future uses of biobank data remain open.

21 E.g. Beauchamp and Childress 2008.
22 See Rose 2009.
23 See also Eurobarometer 2010.
24 Gottweis and Petersen 2008.
25 Knoppers 2010.
26 Gottweis and Lauss 2010.

Uncontrollability of digital information flows was acknowledged by all people in our focus groups. While people accept it, they still exercise privacy management in various forms to control the information flows. In general, people have strong views and self-imposed limits to what they want to share and to protect, and for what purposes. They can have very concrete personal restrictions about sharing pieces of information like personal pictures, social security number or information about family relations. Privacy management is also affected by who collects and uses the information and for what purposes. By self-regulating what you share most people were confident that they could protect their privacy in ICT networks. Self-control thus implies the drawing of the boundaries on a specific content of information and the identification of whom the information is being shared with.[27] In social media, people mould their personal 'profiles' through self-imposed restrictions and priorities. Thus, the person becomes presented in social media primarily through self-control.

Many people in the focus groups were not completely aware of the variety and complexity of acquisition and storage of personal data in ICT networks. They were surprised when other discussants told about the ways Facebook, Amazon or Google gather information about the service users. From this perspective privacy management through self-control seems illusionary.

A strategy alternative to self-control is deployment of second identities. A widely used example in the focus groups is the creation of a second e-mail address when spam or other unwanted information is expected. In Facebook, some people have separate profiles for work and social life. To some, the 'double' allows more active presentation of the self and communication, as the 'real' person is not in danger of being violated. In social media, self-control and second identities enable the construction and shaping of one's personality. Even a totally new biography or social role can be shaped on the Internet. It is also a question of co-shaping the person, as private information is not only shared by oneself but also commented and constructed by others.

Regarding biobanks, self-control or second identities as means of privacy management are limited. Participation in a biobank requires the sharing of predetermined personal information, like genetic or other biological data. The only way one can choose what pieces of vital and personal information to share is not to participate in biobanks, i.e. to opt out. However, it seems that people in Finland and elsewhere in Europe think rather positively about participation in biobanks and do not consider donation of tissue sample and sharing of health information to cause them personal harm.[28] As the individual participants in bi-

27 Petronio 2002; Rössler 2005.

28 Tupasela et al. 2010; Eurobarometer 2010.

obanks are not in control over circulation and deployment of biobank data, *trust* between the donors and institutions collecting and circulating vital information becomes highly important. People in our focus groups demand and expect biobanks to be well controlled. References were made to the Finnish society that is believed to have the registers containing personal data under control rather well. People trust that health information, biobank data included, will not be distributed to third parties or 'wrong hands', and that the biobank data is allowed to be used only for biomedical research. In this context, governance of biobank deposits and privacy policy is about creation and maintenance of trust.[29]

Self formation, being me

In general, the biobank data is being only used for medical research, and the donors do not usually receive directly any information back. However, our focus group studies show that people would like to get some sort of feedback from their participation. The feedback discussed in the groups comprised three types: direct information of personal health and risks; non-personal information about risks factors and diseases based on the aggregated data; and information about what kind of research has been conducted with the biobank data, as people want to know that they have contributed to something good by sharing private information.

People have an ambiguous attitude about receiving information about their personal genetic susceptibility to diseases. Becoming aware of possible genetic risks can influence personal identity and conduct both positively and negatively. Somehow it is regarded to be a personal right to know about the identified genetic risks. It was argued that knowledge of risks enables the person to take control of her or his own life and health. Some people were very interested to know how they could influence their health through life style choices, and concomitantly shape themselves.[30] However, genetic risks were also seen frightening. Knowing personal risks and those of one's children was seen confusing and having potential to hinder the normal cause of life and to affect personal identity.[31] All in all, attitudes towards receiving personal information in a genetic form are ambivalent.[32] DNA samples and other biological material in the biobanks contain a lot of private health information that are tangible to the person only through its deployment in biomedical research, i.e. after researchers and doctors

29 Hoeyer 2012.

30 See Hoeyer 2004; Bloss et al. 2011; Helén 2004b.

31 E.g. Helén 2004a; Koch and Svendsen 2005.

32 See McGuire et al. 2009.

have processed the molecular and digital data and made risk calculations. This genetic risk information may then function as a tool for self-formation, since it provides knowledge about the person that was previously *unknown* to her or him.

Today, among the providers of such information are direct-to-consumer (DTC) genetic tests services on the Internet. They provide a route for feedback from research conducted with biobank data and enable indirectly personalisation of genetic information created with biobanks. DTC companies offer to individual consumers information about their genetic traits and susceptibilities to diseases in a context outside public health care. The customers send a tissue sample to a service provider which makes a molecular analysis of the sample and gives an estimate of genetic health risks of the person on the basis of existing research evidence. Service providers like deCODEme and 23andMe deliver 'genome wide' mappings of the individual's genetic traits and risks, while others like Genecodebook in Finland focus only on specific conditions.

23andMe is one of the most prominent commercial providers DTC tests, in terms of volume and publicity. In its website, the company offers the mapping of personal genome for the price of 99 US$:

> Gain insight into your traits, from baldness to muscle performance. Discover risk factors for 97 diseases. Know your predicted response to drugs, from blood thinners to coffee. And uncover your ancestral origins.

Customers provide DNA samples and fill in voluntary surveys regarding their health. In return they receive a genetic profile that is claimed to cover currently '193 diseases and conditions that cover carrier status, drug response, and disease risk.' Some of the genetic associations are said to be based on established research while others are only based on preliminary studies. Many geneticists and bioethical experts have made cautious and sceptical statements about the utility of DTC genetics. The outputs from DTC tests are risk calculations which can change rapidly due to new reference genomes and biomarkers, or they can be confusing since different DTC companies provide conflicting results on one variable.[33]

The result of genome 'mapping' is a personal profile of risks and susceptibilities to certain diseases. It has been debated whether this kind of information helps individuals to gain control over their health and to make life style choices or whether it may violate their privacy by exposing people to possibly confusing and unwanted information. The information may also be disappointing or even useless to the consumers.[34] 23andMe states in its website that 'We believe that

33 ESHG 2010; Caulfield 2009.

34 Hastings Center Report 40:5 (2010); Richards 2010.

your genetic information should be controlled by you.' This statement gives an impression of consumer empowerment; however, the company commercializes the data it acquires from the customers by selling aggregated genetic and self-reported information for research purposes. Thus, when purchasing a personal genetic risk profile from 23andMe, the customer gives away the control over circulation of vital information she or he has provided.

Digitalized biosociality

People value feedback and actively deploy information, for example in social media. They are willing to share personal information – even genetic data – and participate in information flows, as the information which is shared and received offers opportunities and means for the presentation of the self as well as opportunities to become recognized as a person. Presenting the self, being connected, gathering information about others, and benefiting from information in the cyberspace are about being social.

Current modes of formation of social groups and communities around personal health and biomedical identity are often described as *biosociality*. The concept refers in particular to new patients' activism and networks which are organized as virtual communities in the Internet. They are characterized by strong personal identification to the community on the basis of a specific medical condition, and are actively involved in developing new forms of cure through alliances with research institutions and private medical companies. Biosociality is closely linked with the rise of genomic medicine, which has discovered new disorders, provided a large amount of new information about causes and aetiology of various disorders, and developed techniques to test the person's genetic susceptibility to specific diseases.[35] In their websites, discussion fora and blogs, patients' networks provide opportunities for their members to share information and personal experiences, to present themselves and to acquire means of self-formation. Thus, biosociality is greatly actualized in a digital form, and the basis of identification is bioinformation circulating in the Web. In addition, many patients' networks contribute to the 'tissue economy' by maintaining biobanks. Most of them focus on a single rare disease or a group of them, while Généthon, the most significant biobank in France, is run and ruled by a patients' association.[36] The biobanks run by patients' organisations are in many ways similar to public biobanks, and they do not usually offer personal information back to participants. Thus, they are not able to meet the patient's demand of direct feedback

35 Rabinow 1996; Rose and Novas 2005; Novas 2006; Novas 2008.

36 Novas 2006; Mayrhofer 2008.

information which is provided by, for example, DTC genetics. However, there are modes of action in which circulation of personal health information, advanced biomedical research, and social networking in the cyberspace merge profoundly. An Internet portal PatientsLikeMe is an example of such a fusion. Through its website patients with different medical conditions can share information, and anyone can create a personal profile based on her or his diseases or symptoms. Membership is free and members can update online their profiles of physical and mental condition, communicate with each other, and share experiences of treatments and medications. PatientsLikeMe builds multiple fora for biosociality and connects them through ICT network.[37] In addition, it commercializes biosociality, since the company sells the information provided and shared by patients. PatientsLikeMe states in its website that 'The more you share, the easier it will be to find patients like you.' Sharing of personal health information data is said to benefit the members, as they can find information and contacts relevant to them, and acquire more knowledge about their diseases. Open sharing of information also benefits the company, because it gains more data to be sold to other companies. The way PatientsLikeMe explicitly devalues the idea of privacy resembles the view of Mark Zuckerberg, the CEO of Facebook, who stated that privacy as a social norm has eroded in social media, as people are accustomed to share personal information openly in the Web, 'with friends' and in public.[38] Similarly, the company PatientsLikeMe states that 'We believe privacy has hindered the effective development of new treatments and shared understanding of how to manage disease'. Information sharing is seen as a way to promote common good and personal benefits, but it also works as a means to manage one's own life through the biosocial networks. Besides a compulsory privacy policy, the company has an 'openness philosophy' based on the idea that 'Openness can save lives'. In PatientsLikeMe people can share their health information behind virtual personalities, which do not necessarily need to correspond to the real person. This web portal is a prime example of how individuals present their selves and use 'private' information to connect with others and to gain more knowledge. Similar dimensions of social networking can be found in 23andMe, too. The customers can have access to information about their genetic relatives by using the relative finder function in the website. They may also get contact to discussion fora or blogs of people with similar genetic risk profiles or diseases as themselves.

23andMe and PatientsLikeMe have recently started cooperation for cases of specific diseases. According to the PatientsLikeMe press release:

---

37 See Lee and Crawley 2009.

38 E.g.www.readwriteweb.com/facebooks_zuckerberg_says_the_age_of_privacy_is_ov.php

> PatientsLikeMe is teaming with 23andMe on its effort to recruit 10,000 people with Parkinson's for a massive study of the disease, and give patients a way to learn more about their personal genetics.

Basically, patients are informed of their specific genetic mutation related to Parkinson's disease through 23andMe (or other means) and can update this information in their PatientsLikeMe profile. With this linkage, circulation of social and personal data is increasingly connected to genetic information not only in relation to medical research but also in the digitalized public space.

Unfinished

DTC genetic testing and web portals like PatientsLikeMe are concrete examples of how the flows of DNA and other vital information merge with the broader digital universe. Transnational biobank networks and more intensive global collaboration in biomedical research are already creating the cyberspace of bioinformation, and DTC genetic testing and other forms of consumer genetics are just reinforcing this development.

It is quite likely that the expansion of the flows of bioinformation will bring along problems of uncontrollability in collection and circulation of personal data and uncertainty over protection of informational privacy, similar to the ones encountered with other kind of digitalized personal information. As mediations between donors, aggregators and users of biological data increase, expand globally and become more complex, tracing of the dispersion and uses of the personal samples and information becomes very difficult. In addition, risks of unintended failures in data management and protection due to bureaucratic negligence, disregard or complexity of the governance system increase considerably.[39] In these new settings, the conventional approaches to informational privacy and its protection in medical research and practice seem misplaced and inoperable, and the focal challenge in regulation of collection, sharing and deployment of bioinformation in the digital universe is to define the meanings, limits and safeguards of privacy context by context.[40]

More intensive circulation of vital information in multiple settings in the cyberspace inserts a molecular dimension to the openness of today's digital personhood. As said, mapping the personal genome and presenting a genetic (risk) profile may reveal a person previously unknown and potentially contribute to major life changes. But the meaning of information about a carrier status or genetic susceptibility may change with time, and this change will be strongly af-

39 See Solove 2004.

40 See Nissenbaum 2010.

fected by global circulation of molecular and digital health information between biobanks, genome sequencing laboratories, and research sites. For the person who participates in this circulation as a donor, a patient or a customer, what her or his basic vital characteristics are and how they affect her or his life and the self remain open, essentially unknown and potentially modifiable.

Against this background, informational privacy should be redefined in terms of personal management of vital information which affects the person's self-reflection and self-modification. In this context, informational privacy – control over what other people know about oneself – is a process concept, related to possibilities and abilities of the person to select, share and interpret personal information circulating in the digital universe.

Bibliography

Alastalo, M. and Åkerman, M. (eds.) 2011. *Tieto hallinnassa*. Tampere: Vastapaino.

Beauchamp, T. and Childress, J. 2008. *Principles of Biomedical Ethics*, 6th edition. New York: Oxford University Press.

Bloss, C. S., Ornowski L., Silver, E., Cargill, M., Vanier, V., Schork, N. J., and Topol, E. J. 2011.'Consumer Perceptions of Direct-to-Consumer Personalized Genomic Risk Assessments'. *Genetics in Medicine*, 12, 556-66.

Boyd, D. 2010. 'Social network sites as networked publics: Affordances, Dynamics, and Implications'. In Z. Papacharissi (ed.) *Networked self. Community and culture on social network sites*. London and New York: Routledge, 39-58.

Cambon-Thomsen, A. 2004. 'The social and ethical issues of post-genomic human biobanks'. *Nature Reviews Genetics*, 5, 866-73.

Carrithers, M., Collins, S. and Lukes, S. (eds.) 1987. *The category of the person: Anthropology, philosophy, history*. Cambridge: Cambridge University Press.

Castells, M. 1996. *The rise of network society*. Cambridge, MA: Blackwell.

Caulfield, T. 2009. 'Direct-to-consumer genetics and health policy: A worst-case scenario?'. *American Journal of Bioethics*, 9:6-7, 48-50.

Craig, D., Goor, R., Wang, Z., Paschall J., Ostell, J., Feolo, M., Sherry, S. and Manolio, T. 2011. 'Assessing and managing risk when sharing aggregate genetic variant data'. *Nature Reviews Genetics*, 12, 730-36.

Eurobarometer 2010. Special Eurobarometer 341. Biotechnology.

European Society of Human Genetics (ESHG), 2010. 'Statement of the ESHG on direct-to-consumer genetic testing for health-related purposes'. *European Journal of Human Genetics*, 18, 1271-73.

Goffman, E. 1959. *Presentation of the self in everyday life*. New York: Anchor.

Gottweis, H. and Lauss, G. 2010. 'Biobank governance in the post-genomic age'. *Personalized Medicine*, 7, 1-9.

Gottweis, H. and Petersen, A. (eds.) 2008. *Biobanks. Governance in comparative perspective*. London and New York: Routledge.

Hasting Center Report 40: 5, 2010.

Helén, I. 2004a. 'Technics over life. Risk, ethics and the existential condition in high-tech antenatal care'. *Economy and Society*, 33, 28-51.

Helén, I. 2004b. 'Health in prospect. High-tech medicine, life enhancement and the economy of hope'. *Science Studies*, 17:1, 3-19.

Hirtzlin, I., Dubreuil, C., Préaubert, N., Duchier, J., Jansen, B. et al. 2003. 'An empirical survey on biobanking of human genetic material and data in six EU countries'. *European Journal of Human Genetics*, 11, 475-88.

Hoeyer, K. 2004. 'Ambiguous gifts: Public anxiety, informed consent and biobanks'. In R. Tutton and O. Corrigan (eds.) *Genetic databases: Socio-ethical issues in the collection and use of DNA*. London: Routledge, 97-116.

Hoeyer, K. 2012. 'Trading in cold blood? Trustworthiness in face of commerizialized biobank infrastructures'. In P. Dabrock, J. Tauptz and J. Reid (eds.) *Trust in biobanking*. Berlin: Springer, 21-42.

Kaye, J. and Stranger, M. (eds.) 2009. *Principles and practice in biobank governance*. Farnham: Ashgate.

Koch, L. and Svendsen M. 2005. 'Providing solution – defining problems: The imperative of disease prevention in genetic counselling'. *Social Science and Medicine*, 60, 823-32.

Knoppers, B. 2010. 'Consent to "personal" genomics and privacy'. *EMBO reports*, 11, 416-19.

Lee, S. S. and Crawley, L. 2009. 'Research 2.0: Social networking and direct-to-consumer (DTC) genomics'. *American Journal of Bioethics*, 9: 6-7, 35-44.

Mayrhofer, M. 2008. 'Patient organizations as the (un)usual suspects. The biobanking activities of the Association Francaise contre les Myopathies and its Généthon DNA and cell bank'. In H. Gottweis and A. Petersen (eds.) *Biobanks. Governance in comparative perspective*. London and New York: Routledge, 71-87.

McGuire, A. L., Diaz, C. M., Wang, T. and Hilsenbeck, S. G. 2009. 'Social networkers' attitudes toward direct-to-consumer personal genome testing'. *American Journal of Bioethics*, 9:6-7, 3-10.

McKee, A. 2005. *The public sphere. An introduction*. Cambridge and New York: Cambridge University Press.

Nissenbaum, H. 2010. *Privacy in context. Technology, policy, and the integrity of social life*. Stanford: Stanford University Press.

Novas, C. 2006. 'The political economy of hope. Patients' organizations, science and biovalue'. *BioSocieties*, 1, 289-305.

Novas C. 2008. 'Patients, profits and values. Myozyme as an exemplar of biosociality'. In S. Gibbon and C. Novas (eds.) *Biosocialities, genetics and the social sciences*. London: Routledge, 136-56.

Papacharissi, Z. (ed.), 2010. *Networked self. Community and culture on social network sites*. London and New York: Routledge.

Petronio, S. 2002. *Boundaries of privacy*. Albany: State University of New York Press.

Rabinow, P. 1996. *Essays on the anthropology of reason*. Princeton: Princeton University Press.

Richards, M. 2010. 'Reading the runs of my genome: A personal exploration of retail genetics'. *New Genetics and Society*, 29, 291-310.

Rose, N. 2009. 'Normality and pathology in a biomedical age'. *The Sociological Review*, 57, 66-83.

Rose, N. and Novas, C. 2005. 'Biological citizenship'. In A. Ong and S. J. Collier (eds.) *Global assemblages*. Malden: Blackwell, 439-63.

Rössler, B. 2005. *The value of privacy*. Cambridge: Polity.

Solove, D. 2004. *The digital person*. New York & London: New York University Press.

Tupasela, A., Sihvo S., Snell, K., Jallinoja, P., Aro, A. R. and Hemminki, E. 2010. 'Attitudes towards the biomedical use of tissue sample collections, consent and biobanks among Finns'. *Scandinavian Journal of Public Health*, 38, 46-54.

Waldby, C. and Mitchell, R. 2006. *Tissue economies*. Durham and London: Duke University Press.

Warren, S. and Brandeis, L. 1890. 'The right to privacy'. *Harvard Law Review*, 4, 193-220.

Waters, S. and Ackerman, J. 2011. 'Exploring privacy management on Facebook: Motivations and perceived consequences of voluntary disclosure'. *Journal of Computer-Mediated Communication*, 17, 101-15.

Notes on Contributors

Margherita Carucci was a research fellow at the Helsinki Collegium for Advanced Studies, Finland. She has published a book on *The Romano-African domus: studies in space, decoration, and function* (2007) along with a number of articles on a variety of aspects of the Graeco-Roman society, such as visual art, gender studies, and urbanism, with particular focus on social and cultural history. Her current specific interest is on every aspect related to the domestic experience in the Roman society that she explores with the support of modern critical theories in sociology, anthropology, media, and art history.

Maryanne Dever is an Associate Professor in the School of Humanities and Social Science at the University of Newcastle, Australia. She was formally Director of the Centre for Women's Studies & Gender Research at Monash University in Melbourne. Her current research examines issues of intimacy and materiality, with particular reference to private correspondence held in public repositories. Her most recent co-authored book is *The Intimate Archive: Journeys Through Private Papers* (National Library of Australia, 2009).

Stephan Dudeck is an anthropologist currently working at the Arctic Centre of the University of Lapland in Rovaniemi, Finland. In 2008- 2011 he was a research fellow in the Siberian Studies Centre, Max Planck Institute for Social Anthropology, Germany. Since 1999 he has been working as a free lance ethnographer for different documentary films and NGOs. His fields of interests are conditions of lifestyle diversification, neo-traditionalism and nativistic movements, relations between taiga and town, adaptation to technological change, practices of hiding and avoidance, oil-production and indigenous peoples, language and education policies, and visual anthropology.

Ilpo Helén is Professor of Science and Technology Studies and Adjunct Professor of Sociology in the Department of Social Research at the University of Helsinki. His studies on history and current trends of Western medical biopolitics have focused on, for example, abortions and sexual health, medical maternity care, prenatal diagnosis, health and welfare policy and mental health care. Currently, he is studying the mutual influences of knowledge, technology and health care practices in the area of medical high-tech, especially in genomics and neurosciences.

Karol Kurnicki is a PhD candidate in the Institute of Sociology at the Jagiellonian University in Kraków, Poland. His main areas of interests are urban sociology, urban studies, critical sociology and applied social sciences. In his doctoral dissertation, 'Ideologies in a city. On social production of urban space', he analyses contemporary urban ideas and ideologies and their influence on local policies, economies and social practice.

Elena Liarskaia is an anthropologist currently working at the European University of Saint Petersburg, Russia. In 2007-2010 she was a research fellow in the Siberian Studies Centre, Max Planck Institute for Social Anthropology (Germany). Since 1997 she has done extensive ethnographic and archival fieldwork in St. Petersburg, Russia, and in the Yamal Nenets Autnomous District. Her fields of interests are transformation of native culture in the Far North, family and the position of women among the small-numbered indigenous peoples of the North, interaction of Northern peoples'cultures with the European civilization, and anthropology of education.

Linda McGuire teaches courses at the Institut d'Études politiques de Paris and the Burgundy School of Business in Dijon, France. Her current interest in Cicero's Letters to Atticus stems from ongoing research into the way elite Roman women accessed and used different forms of wealth and its impact on their role in society. She is a member of the Women's History Network and the Society for the Promotion of Roman studies.

Sarah Parsons is an Associate Professor in the Department of Visual Arts at York University in Toronto, Canada, where she teaches the history and theory of photography. Her recent publications include 'Public/Private Tensions in the Photography of Sally Mann', *History of Photography* (2008) and 'Sontag's Lament: Emotion, Ethics, and Photography', *Photography & Culture* (2009).

Floora Ruokonen is the Head of Planning and Development at the Helsinki Collegium for Advanced Studies. She has also worked as a Science Adviser at the Academy of Finland and as a Lecturer and researcher at the Department of Social and Moral Philosophy at the University of Helsinki. She has published articles on the relationship of ethics and aesthetics, the history of philosophy, and the philosophy of trust.

Katarzyna Salamon has graduated from Jagiellonian University in Kraków, Poland, in sociology and philosophy. She wrote her PhD thesis under the supervision of Prof Krzysztof Frysztacki in the Jagiellonian University. She is especially interested in the social work theory, social identity, professional identity, professional ethic, and communication in groups. She is an author of many publications.

Kris W. B. Scheerlinck studied Architecture (KUL/WENK, School of Architecture, Campus Sint-Lucas, Gent), Spatial Planning (University of Gent/Leuven) and Urban Design (UPC Barcelona) and obtained his doctoral degree in Architecture and Urban Projects with Prof. de Solà-Morales and Prof. Ferrer as thesis directors (UPC/URL Barcelona). He runs studios and teaches in international Architecture and Urban Design Programs at various institutions and universities in New York, Barcelona, Gent and Brussels, where he continues academic research on depth configurations in urban projects. He is currently Head of Master Programs in Architecture at the KUL/WENK, School of Architecture, Campus Sint-Lucas.

Karoliina Snell is a postdoctoral researcher in the Department of Social Research at the University of Helsinki. In her research in sociology of science and technology she has approached biotechnology and biomedicine from different angles. She has studied, for example, social responsibility in developing new technologies and public opinion about biomedicine. She is currently working in an international PrivateGen consortium focusing on privacy and biobanks.

Miia Vistilä is a soon to be Master of Social Sciences from the University of Helsinki. Her main academic interest is on questions of privacy in the Internet. She is also a comic artist publishing her comic strips in journals and in her own blog.